ALL ABOUT BRITAIN

This book tells the story of the people who have lived in the
British Isles, and is packed with fascinating facts and fun tales.
The British Isles is a group of islands that consists of two main
islands – Great Britain and Ireland – and lots of smaller islands,
including the Isle of Man, the Orkney Islands, the Shetland Islands,
the Isles of Scilly, the Isle of Wight and the Channel Islands.

The UNITED KINGDOM is
made up of Great Britain
(England, Scotland, and Wales)
and Northern Ireland.

SCOTLAND

Edinburgh

NORTH SEA

NORTHERN
IRELAND

Belfast

IRISH SEA

Dublin
THE REPUBLIC
OF IRELAND

ENGLAND

WALES

Cardiff

London

The Republic of Ireland
is a separate nation from
the United Kingdom.

ENGLISH CHANNEL

Before and After

Some of the dates in this book have the letters BC or AD written
beside them. BC means 'Before Christ' and is used to describe
the time before the birth of Jesus (the Christian son of God).
AD stands for *Anno Domini*, a Latin phrase meaning 'in the year of
our Lord'. It is used to describe the time after the birth of Christ.
In this book, all dates after AD 400 are written without AD.

7

PREHISTORIC TIMES

THE ANCIENT BRITONS
500,000 BC – 700 BC

The term prehistoric means the time before people wrote down accounts of what happened. This isn't because they were lazy, but because writing hadn't been invented yet. To discover what life was really like, historians have to rely on archaeology (the study of remains from the past). Today, archaeologists agree that prehistoric Britain can be divided up into four main Ages.

The Ice Age

Around 700,000 years ago, the area we now call Europe was a big, icy land mass. People moved around on it, following animals which they hunted for food. When the ice started to melt, the sea levels rose and the islands of Britain were formed. The people who arrived on these islands are called ancient Britons.

The Stone Age

From around 12,000 years ago, the ancient Britons began using stones to make axes and animal skins to make shelters. Groups of people began to settle in one spot, and from around 6,000 years ago they began to plant crops and breed animals.

The Bronze Age

From around 3000 BC, bronze metal was used to make tools and weapons, instead of stone and flint.

The Iron Age

From around 1000 BC, bronze tools and weapons were replaced by stronger, iron ones. More effective weapons meant that groups of people formed into tribes led by a powerful chief, and built hilltop forts to live in.

BUILDING STONEHENGE
Built 3100 BC – 1100 BC

The early Britons were so good at building structures from stone that some are still standing today. No one really knows what these strange structures were used for, but many archaeologists believe they were made to celebrate the changing seasons or to worship the sun.

Stonehenge is a prehistoric structure, found in Wiltshire, that is made up of a ring of vertical slabs of stone. Here is a brief history of the three main phases of its construction.

Stonehenge I

By around 3100 BC, people using deer antlers to break the earth dug a ditch about 2 metres deep and roughly 6 metres wide, forming a circle 98 metres across. Two tall stones marked the entrance on the northeast side of the circle. A wooden henge (which means a circular area) may also have been built at this time.

Stonehenge II

A bigger and better henge was built around 2300 BC. About 80 stones, each weighing up to four tonnes, were placed upright in the centre of the site, forming another two circles. The stones were brought about 380 kilometres from a quarry in Wales – but no one really knows how. Many of the stones were carefully angled to line up with the position of the sun at different times of the year.

Stonehenge III

Around 2000 BC, more work was carried out and a new circle, with a horseshoe-shape of large stones, was created. A ring of

30 upright stones, weighing up to 50 tonnes each and standing up to 9 metres tall, were added, and these were connected by a ring of stones that were laid on top.

For the next thousand years, people continued adding to the structure. Today the whole site is about 5 kilometres across, and includes routes along which processions took place and several barrows (which are ancient burial sites).

Stonehenge is probably the most famous structure that survives from prehistoric times, but there are others. Silbury Hill, in Wiltshire, England, is the largest prehistoric mound of earth in Europe, and would have taken over ten years to build.

COURAGEOUS CELTS
Around 650 BC

Around 650 BC, groups of people from Eastern Europe, known as Celts, arrived on the southern shores of Britain. Unable to defend their homes, the ancient Britons were forced to accept Celtic rule.

The Celtic warriors had some seriously bloodthirsty habits, which included cutting off the heads of resident Britons, not just to kill them, which of course it did, but because the Celts believed they would gain their victims' courage, strength and intelligence. The Celtic kings consulted religious advisors to help them rule, known as druids. They gave the druids many gifts, which may have included people, to sacrifice in order to please their gods.

Poetic Superstars

As well as a love of spilling blood, the Celts were huge fans of poetry. Poets were treated like superstars, and had to train for over ten years, learning hundreds of long and exciting stories which they would recite to crowds of eager listeners.

THE ROMANS INVADE
AD 43

The Roman Empire was a vast area of land, ruled by a series of powerful, land-hungry leaders. So it wasn't long before Rome's rulers began to look greedily across at the lush green isle where the Britons lived…

The Romans Invade

To the Romans, Britain was a territory rich in gold, bronze and iron, defended only by a bunch of funny-looking 'barbarians'. It didn't matter how civilized or refined you were, anyone who wasn't a Roman was called a barbarian.

Julius Caesar, the Roman commander, thought that the Britons were a primitive people who 'dyed their skins blue with woad' (a natural dye), because they believed it made them look more fearsome in battle. Equipped with the advanced military techniques of the Roman army, Caesar thought that the Britons and their warpaint would be an easy conquest.

Caesar launched two invasions along the coast of Britain, the first in 55 BC and then again a year later. To the Romans' dismay, the local Britons managed to fend off the first invasion and Caesar had to abandon the second to deal with a revolt in France. But, almost one hundred years later, an Emperor of Rome named Claudius sent troops to try again.

In AD 43, around 40,000 of Claudius' troops landed on Britain's southern shores. The army swept north and west, defeating the Britons on battlefields across the country. When some Britons retreated to their hilltop forts, the Romans used huge catapults to fire boulders and bolts to topple the strongholds. Within seven years, many Britons had surrendered.

The Romans named their newly conquered territory Britannia. The conquered people of Britain were offered *Pax Romana* (which means 'Roman Peace' in Latin). They could live in peace as long as they paid money, known as taxes, to the Romans. This system was so successful that it enabled the Romans to remain in control of much of Britain for the next 400 years.

Roman Rewards

Among other important things, such as bringing law and order to Britain's towns and villages, the Romans introduced really useful things such as toilets and even vegetables to the people of Britain. The Romans also shared their building know-how. Public baths were heated by hot pipes running under the floors, and the Romans built a network of roads that still form the basis for many roads that we travel on today. Unfortunately for the resident Britons, Romans liked to build straight roads, and demolished whatever lay in the way.

HURRY UP, OR THE COW GETS IT!

THE BIRTH OF LONDINIUM
—————— AD 50 ——————

When the Romans arrived, the area on which London stands today was just a piece of marshy ground with a few farms built on it. The Romans quickly recognized the advantages of the land being next to a large river, the River Thames, which boats could sail up to load and unload their goods. They began building a town, London, which they called *Londinium*.

Merchants, traders and other townsfolk quickly moved to the new site, and London soon took over from Camulodunum (now called Colchester) as the biggest town in Britain.

Trouble in the City

London grew rapidly for the next few years, and many (perfectly straight) roads were constructed to connect it with the rest of the country. However, in the year AD 60, it was destroyed by fire and its citizens slaughtered by a rival tribe whose leader was a Briton named Queen Boudicca (see pages 18 to 19).

After about 20 years, London began to recover, and it grew quickly into a bustling centre for trade and business. By around AD 120, it became the headquarters of Roman Britain. Its richer inhabitants built splendid villas to live in, a large town hall and an amphitheatre (which is a building with curved rows of seating facing an area in the middle where performances took place).

To protect London against another invasion, a massive stone wall was built around its edges in around AD 200, guarded by soldiers to keep out any barbarians who might want to wander in.

THE ROMANS AND CHRISTIANITY
From AD 200s

Throughout the centuries of Roman rule in Britain, the Christian religion had been steadily spreading across Europe from the Middle East. However, in the beginning, the Romans really didn't like Christians, and in Rome they would sometimes flog, imprison and kill people who followed Christianity and refused to worship Roman gods. Some Christians were even fed to lions.

The Story of Saint Alban

A similarly unpleasant fate befell a Roman soldier named Alban, when he offered shelter to a Christian priest who was fleeing Roman persecution. After listening to the priest's stories about his religion, Alban was so impressed that he converted to Christianity himself. When Roman soldiers came looking for the priest, Alban tried to protect him by pretending to be the priest they were after. When the soldiers realized the deception, Alban was executed. He was later made a saint, and his home town in England was renamed Saint Albans in his honour.

Christians were not protected from persecution by law until AD 313.

YOU LOOK JUST LIKE A ROMAN SOLDIER ... THEY WON'T SUSPECT A THING.

BOUDICCA'S REVOLT
Died AD 60/61

Despite bringing useful things to Britain, such as law and order and warm baths, not everyone was pleased to see the Romans arrive. The Celtic tribes living in Britain at the time were proud warriors who loved their country – and none more so than the Iceni, a tribe that lived in what is now Norfolk.

The Iceni were ruled by the powerful King Prasutagus. The conquering Romans asked him to remain king in order to help keep the peace. He agreed on one condition – that when he died, his inheritance would be split between his family and Nero, a Roman Emperor.

The Romans happily agreed to his request when Prasutagus was alive, but as soon as he died, in AD 60, Nero decided he wasn't satisfied with his share of land and broke his promise. His army invaded the town where the Iceni lived, looting and publicly flogging Queen Boudicca, King Prasutagus' wife.

Boudicca, a fearsome woman described as having 'eyes that seemed to stab you, a voice harsh and loud, (and) thick reddish-brown hair that hung down', was fighting mad. She gathered a huge army of Iceni tribesmen and launched an attack on the

cities we know today as Colchester, St Albans and London. In London, the Iceni smashed their way through the city walls, slaughtering the population and burning buildings to the ground.

The Roman governor of Britain, named Paulinus, decided swift action should be taken to get rid of the troublesome Boudicca. He gathered a force of 10,000 soldiers, and set off to confront her. The Romans knew they were outnumbered by at least ten to one, so they cleverly took up positions in a narrow clearing between two forests, and prepared themselves for attack.

From her chariot, Boudicca led her tribe into battle, pushing her huge numbers of men forwards into the Roman line. However, the tightly packed, highly disciplined Roman soldiers very quickly cut the Iceni to pieces and won the battle. By the end of the battle, 80,000 of Boudicca's men lay dead.

Bad Luck Boudicca

As for Boudicca, no one knows her exact fate. Some people claim she took poison, others think that she died of a disease. However it happened, the result was the same for the defeated Queen of the Iceni – death.

WHAT DO YOU MEAN I'M THE SCARIEST WOMAN YOU'VE EVER MET?

HADRIAN'S WALL
AD 122 – 130

By around AD 100, the Romans had conquered most of Britain … apart from Scotland. In a bid to rule the whole island, the Romans repeatedly tried to invade Scotland, but the Scottish soldiers kept fighting back. From time to time, they even tried to invade Roman Britain themselves.

To solve the problem, a Roman Emperor named Hadrian ordered a huge wall to be built – to protect Roman borders and separate the Scottish 'barbarians' from the 'civilized' people in Roman Britain. When it was finished, the wall, now known as Hadrian's Wall, stretched across the whole of the north of England. It measured a whopping 118 kilometres, from one coast of Britain to the other, and was the largest stone structure ever built in the Roman Empire.

This amazing feat of engineering took more than six years to complete, using over three million tonnes of stone and the skills of hundreds of people. Along its length were forts guarded by soldiers.

The wall was used for defence until the Romans left Britain for good.

ROMAN RULE COLLAPSES
409

Despite the *Pax Romana*, or Roman Peace, life in Roman Britain was never that peaceful. Roman settlers had to struggle against invaders from abroad and rebels at home who wanted to seize power for themselves.

In AD 180, tribes from Scotland tried to invade Roman Britain, hoping to increase their own territories. Then in AD 287, a Roman admiral named Carausius rebelled and attempted to seize power to become the ruler of an independent Britain. In both these cases, the Roman army managed to crush the troublemakers.

Attacked from all Sides

In AD 367, however, the Romans faced a number of more serious threats to their control. Two tribes, known as the Picts from Scotland and the Scots from Ireland, managed to invade Roman Britain.

At the same time, the Roman Empire was coming under attack on all sides by a collection of new enemies. These included rebel tribes in Britain and tribes in Europe called Angles, Jutes and Saxons from areas now known as Germany and Denmark. This constant fighting took its toll on the Romans who lived in Britain.

Finally, in the year 409, a Roman Emperor named Honorius pulled the remaining Roman troops out of Britain, taking them to fight enemy tribes who were threatening the Empire closer to Rome. This marks the end of Roman rule in Britain.

THE EARLY
MIDDLE AGES

ANGLO-SAXON SUCCESS

Around 450

After the Romans left in the year 409, Britain was not a very peaceful place to be. Cities were sacked and people were murdered, as tribes from both inside and outside the British Isles battled for land and loot.

Tribes called the Jutes, Angles and Saxons from areas now known as Scandinavia and Germany invaded Britain. One Briton, a warlord named Vortigern (known as the 'proud tyrant'), is even said to have invited Saxons over from Germany to help him fend off the Picts who were invading from Scotland. Unfortunately, they revolted against Vortigern, and instead of returning home after driving back the Picts, the invaders brought more of their tribe over and made themselves at home in the southeast of England.

By the 600s, the Anglo-Saxons were firmly established as the top dogs throughout England. They built large halls for each of their leaders across the country. The halls were protected from rival tribes by nobles called thegns (pronounced 'thaynes').

IF YOUR NAME'S NOT ON THE LIST, YOU'RE NOT COMING IN.

23

King Of The Mercians

In the year 757, an Anglo-Saxon named Offa became king of an area called Mercia (the part of England now called the Midlands). Offa and his army successfully conquered the territories of Sussex, East Anglia, Kent and Essex. Offa became the most powerful Saxon leader and was called 'king of all England'.

Offa had a problem, however. As the Anglo-Saxons had dominated the southeast of England, they had driven the Celts (who had occupied these lands before) westward. Many of the Celts were forced to live in the area we now know as Wales, but they kept trying to fight back.

To solve this big Celt-shaped problem, King Offa ordered a huge bank of earth to be built, with a ditch on one side to keep out the invaders. It was a whopping 270 kilometres long and became known as Offa's Dyke. Parts of the ditch can still be seen today.

During his reign, Offa strengthened relationships with the leaders of other European countries, and brought riches and peace to Britain. When he died in the year 796, however, Anglo-Saxon rule began to face problems, as old rivals attacked and new enemies invaded.

Did You Know?

Many of the names of England's shires, counties and towns come from the Anglo-Saxons. If the name of your town or village ends in '-ton', '-wick', '-worth', '-burn', '-bridge', '-hurst', '-den' or '-ham', it was probably named by the Anglo-Saxons.

Tiw, Woden, Thor and Friya, who were among the many gods Anglo-Saxons worshipped, gave their names to four days of the week – Tuesday, Wednesday, Thursday and Friday.

SAINT PATRICK
Born in the late 5th century

Patrick was born into a wealthy family during the fifth century, somewhere in Britain. His life was fairly uneventful, until one day, when he was 16, he was kidnapped, taken to Ireland, and sold as a slave. After spending six long years working as a shepherd, Patrick turned to Christianity to give him the strength to cope with his hard life. Eventually he managed to escape his captors by stowing away on a boat.

Patrick's Dream Of Ireland

Back home in Britain, Patrick had a dream in which the people of Ireland spoke to him, saying, 'We appeal to you, holy servant boy, to come and walk among us.' He began to train to become a Christian priest and went back to Ireland, where he dedicated his life to converting the Irish people to Christianity.

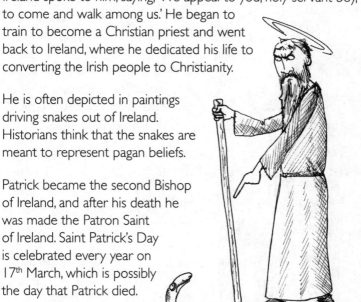

He is often depicted in paintings driving snakes out of Ireland. Historians think that the snakes are meant to represent pagan beliefs.

Patrick became the second Bishop of Ireland, and after his death he was made the Patron Saint of Ireland. Saint Patrick's Day is celebrated every year on 17th March, which is possibly the day that Patrick died.

THE VENERABLE BEDE
673 – 735

In the centuries after the Romans left, the people of Britain were too busy, either fighting each other or defending themselves against invasion, to write down much information.

Little would be known about life in early times without the work of Britain's first historian – a man named Bede who was born towards the end of the seventh century. Bede grew up in a Benedictine monastery at Jarrow, in the northeast of England. He loved writing stuff down and wrote more than 60 books in his lifetime.

One day, Bede had the 'venerable' (which means worthy) idea of recording the first history of the British Isles. He began from the moment that Julius Caesar first invaded Britain, and continued right up to his own time. This impressive work was called *The Ecclesiastical History of the English People*, and he completed it in 731.

To describe the passage of time, he used the BC and AD system, which historians still use today.

For his amazing contribution to British history, Bede is known as the 'Father of English history'.

VIKING INVASION
Around 800

On a clear day in 793, on the Isle of Lindisfarne off the coast of
Northumbria, three strange-looking ships were spotted on the
horizon. With surprising speed and skill, the boats landed on the
beach and hundreds of armed men climbed out.

For the next few decades, the Vikings (as they are now known)
repeatedly sailed over from Scandinavia, in northern Europe.
They came in huge wooden boats called longboats, and staged
sudden, deadly raids along the coastal areas of the British Isles.
The Vikings targeted monasteries in particular, looting the rich
treasures and murdering the
monks they found there.

BROTHER CUTHBERT,
PLEASE COULD YOU TELL
THOSE NICE VIKINGS THE
MONASTERY IS ONLY
OPEN FOR VISITORS
ON THURSDAYS.

Over time, the raids became more frequent until, in 865, the Vikings launched a large invasion of the British Isles. The Anglo-Saxons ruling at the time were divided and disorganized, and were easy prey to the well-armed Vikings. The Vikings conquered much of the north and east of England, along with areas on the Irish and Scottish coasts. They conquered cities to use for trading, such as Jorvik (now called York).

Things were going well for the Vikings, who were led by the terrifying warlord Guthrum, until they came up against King Alfred of Wessex. Alfred's army was beaten many times but eventually managed to crush the Vikings. Guthrum and Alfred were forced to make an agreement. Alfred would rule the west of England, while the east became known as Danelaw and was ruled by the Vikings.

Old habits die hard, however, and the Vikings remained a serious threat for the next couple of centuries, threatening to attack across the borders if they weren't paid money. King Aethelred of England (often referred to as Aethelred the Unready because he was poorly advised by his councillors) raised money by a tax known as Danegeld and paid the Vikings regularly to keep the peace. When Vikings began to settle in areas outside the Danelaw, Aethelred ordered that they should be massacred. Viking leader Swein Forkbeard decided to take revenge and in 1013 he managed to take control of the whole of England.

Did You Know?

The Vikings introduced expertise in ship-building and seafaring that helped Britain win many victories at sea in later years.

CANUTE THE GREAT

Around 990 – 1035 (Crowned 1016)

After the deaths of both the Viking King Swein Forkbeard and the old Saxon King Aethelred, Britain was in desperate need of a ruler to take control. A bloody power struggle commenced between Swein's son, Canute, and Aethelred's son, Edmund Ironside. Eventually, Edmund died in 1016, and Canute was crowned king of England.

Many people in Britain didn't think Canute should be king, however, and were scared of the mighty new ruler. He eventually became a popular ruler by allowing the people to keep the Anglo-Saxon laws they were used to, and he gave generously to the Church.

Canute and the Sea

A story was supposedly spread in which Canute had had enough of being told how powerful he was by his nobles. In order to prove his powers had limits, he stood on the beach and ordered the tide to retreat. After getting wet, the King declared that his powers were limited because God was the only true ruler. Canute then reportedly threw off his crown and never wore it again.

> I'LL RUST IF HE DOESN'T HURRY UP.

29

THE BATTLE OF HASTINGS
1066

After Canute's death, in 1035, his sons, Harold I and Hardicanute, each ruled briefly. Then, in 1042, an Anglo-Saxon man became king of England. He was known as Edward the Confessor because of his devotion to God and his generosity to the poor.

Unfortunately, Edward died in 1066 without children, and three men rushed to stake their claim to his throne. There was a Viking named Harald Hardrada, an Englishman named Harold Godwinson, and a Norman (a person from Normandy, on the north coast of France), named William.

Let the Battles Begin ...

Harold Godwinson declared himself king of England, and set off to defeat Harald Hardrada's army who were invading in the North. In 1066, they met at the Battle of Stamford Bridge, in Yorkshire. The Vikings were defeated and Harald Hardrada was killed.

The Battle of Hastings

The victorious Harold Godwinson had little time to celebrate.
Word soon reached him that William's Norman army had
landed on the south coast of Britain. Harold quickly gathered an
army of 7,000 men, many of whom were completely untrained,
and set off to fight William. The armies met near Hastings.

Harold's men took up a defensive
position on a hill. They made a
wall with their shields.

Harold's troops
seemed to be having some
success in the fighting. But then
they made a fatal error. They
mistakenly thought the Normans were
retreating, so they separated and charged
after them. The Normans turned and quickly cut
down the now scattered English soldiers, winning the battle.

Harold Godwinson was killed on the battlefield, and William of
Normandy was crowned king of England.

Did You Know?

Many people think that Harold was killed at the Battle of
Hastings by an arrow in his eye. A famous tapestry called the
Bayeux Tapestry appears to show Harold dying from this
terrible injury.

31

THE LATER MIDDLE AGES

WILLIAM THE CONQUEROR
1027/8 – 1087 (Crowned 1066)

Having won the English throne at the Battle of Hastings, William of Normandy, now known as William the Conqueror, quickly set about establishing his power throughout the land.

A Norman Takeover

He began his rule by ruthlessly putting down rebellions. In 1069, he punished rebels in the North so severely he is said to have set huge areas of land on fire. The area was so devastated, over 100,000 people were left to starve to death.

William made new laws to try to keep his new English subjects under control. He abolished hanging as a punishment, and criminals had parts of their body cut off and their eyes put out instead. Much nicer!

In the late 1070s, William started building a huge tower by the River Thames, known then as the White Tower (it later became the Tower of London). William filled the tower with guards to defend him against 'the huge and fierce' population of London.

William then took English land and gave it to his Norman barons (powerful members of the nobility). In return, the barons provided knights to fight for the King. Knights were trained warriors who fought on horseback in heavy armour.

Castles were built up and down the country for the barons and their knights to live in. These became symbols of Norman power. The first castles were made up of mounds of earth called mottes, with wooden towers on top surrounded by walled enclosures called baileys – that's why they are known as motte and bailey castles. The towers and walls were later rebuilt in stone.

THE DOMESDAY BOOK
1086

To fund his army and defend his crown, William the Conqueror needed lots of money. He decided the best way to get hold of this was to tax people according to the value of their land. Anxious to find out how much his new kingdom was worth, William commissioned a complete survey of England.

A Survey of Shires

He sent his men out into every shire to find out how many hides (units) of land each person owned. The King's officers met the people of each village and asked every man who had owned the land since the time of Edward the Confessor (who had been king of England until 1066). They also counted how many meadows, mills, ponds and woodlands there were.

It took a whole year to complete the survey and, according to the Anglo-Saxon Chronicle (a record of events made once a year), '… so very strictly did William investigate all the lands that not a yard of land, nor indeed one ox, nor one cow, nor one pig was left out'. Not surprisingly, the survey was very unpopular among the British people. They objected to the nosey King's men, and some people rioted.

All the information collected from William's survey was written down in a book. The English later named it the Domesday Book, because it was thought to be as detailed as the assessment of someone's life that God makes on Judgement Day (also known as Domesday). The Domesday Book survives to this day, and is a fascinating source for historians as it mentions more than 260,000 individual people and more than 13,000 towns, villages and hamlets throughout England.

HENRY II

1133 – 1189 (Crowned 1154)

When William the Conqueror died in 1087, his lands were divided among his children, who squabbled over the crown. The question of who would rule next continued to cause problems for some time. Then, in 1154, William's great-grandson Henry II was crowned king of England. He quickly set about restoring law and order, and built up a vast empire that combined England with a large area of France.

Henry tried to gain control over the English Church by appointing one of his close friends and advisors, a man named Thomas Becket, to the position of the Archbishop of Canterbury. Becket, however, soon became more loyal to the Pope (the head of the Catholic Church in Rome), and Henry and Becket argued furiously.

Deadly Whispers

One day, in 1170, Henry exclaimed in a fit of rage, 'Will no one rid me of this turbulent priest?' Unfortunately, four knights overheard this and mistook his meaning. They rode off to Canterbury and murdered Becket in his cathedral. When Henry found out, he felt very guilty and went barefoot to the site of the murder, wearing only a sackcloth. He begged forgiveness from God while being flogged as a punishment.

RICHARD I 'THE LIONHEART'
1157 – 1199 (Crowned 1189)

When Henry II died, the throne passed to his son, Richard Coeur de Lion (which means Heart of a Lion). He was given this nickname because of his enormous physical strength and for his success in battles.

Richard's greatest ambition was to fight in the Crusades (a series of religious wars fought in the Middle East between Christians and Muslims beginning in the eleventh century). To raise enough money to take his army to recapture Jerusalem from the Muslims, Richard sold as many possessions as he could. He declared that he would sell the city of London if he could find anyone to buy it.

Richard's Relentless Battles

Richard did indeed raise enough money and left England for the Holy Land. He did not return for five years. In fact, during his ten-year reign, he spent less than six months in England. He didn't even bother to learn English properly, preferring to speak in his native tongue – French.

RICHARD'S DISASTROUS JOURNEY HOME ...

OH NO, I AM DOOMED!

Despite his excellent military skills, Richard failed to win back Jerusalem for the Christians, and set off home to England. On his journey, however, things didn't exactly go to plan. First, he was shipwrecked off the coast of Italy. Then, he was captured by Duke Leopold of Austria and imprisoned in a tower. The Duke promised to release the King, but only if an enormous ransom of £100,000 was paid.

Surprisingly, despite his neglect of England, Richard was much-loved among his subjects, and the ransom money was raised. Released from the tower, Richard returned to England, but immediately set off again to reclaim his territory in Normandy, France. While trying to seize the Castle of Châlus, a crossbow bolt pierced Richard's chain-mail armour, and he died ten days later from an infection in the wound.

37

KING JOHN
1167 – 1216 (Crowned 1199)

While Richard the Lionheart is considered one of the greatest English kings, his younger brother, King John, is remembered as a loser. Compared to Richard's countless successes on the battlefields, John had many military failures. One writer at the time even nicknamed him John Softsword.

During his brother's rule, John tried desperately to make himself king. He even attempted to avoid paying the £100,000 ransom needed for Richard's release (see page 37). When Richard returned safely to England, John's scheming didn't stop. A rumour spread that he murdered his own nephew, Arthur, who was a rival of his. It was said that John killed Arthur while drunk and 'possessed by the devil' and disposed of the body in the River Seine in Paris, France.

When Richard died, a joyous John was crowned king in 1199. However, his reign did not start off well. He lost large areas of land to the French. Then, he lost the support of the Church, because he refused to accept the Pope's choice of Archbishop of Canterbury. In order to fund his failing wars abroad, John raised taxes, and this lost him the support of many barons. The barons had had enough and started a civil war (which means a war waged between people who live in the same nation).

Magna Carta

In an effort to stop the fighting, a small group of barons wrote an agreement in 1215, known as Magna Carta. It was designed to limit the King's powers and force him to obey the law. It also protected the barons against unfair taxes and guaranteed all free men of England the right to fair trials. To please his people and because the barons forced him to, King John reluctantly signed

Magna Carta, but he refused to obey the terms it had set out. These actions soon plunged the country into civil war, again.

John's Losing Streak

In 1216, Prince Louis of France was invited by the barons to invade England, and he soon captured London. King John fled, but on his journey, it is said that his luggage carriage became bogged down in quicksand. The crown jewels fell out and disappeared, never to be seen again.

A few months later, the King fell ill – reportedly as a result of eating too many peaches and drinking too much cider (although it is more likely he died from a long-term illness). To the relief of most people in Britain, King John died in October 1216, leaving the throne to his nine-year-old son, who was crowned Henry III.

EDWARD I AND PARLIAMENT
1239 – 1307 (Crowned 1274)

Edward I was nicknamed Longshanks because he was 1.89 metres tall – which is 6 foot 2 inches – and that was quite a height in his day. He was a great warrior and, as a young man, left England to fight in the Crusades. On his way back to England from a battle, he learnt that his father had died, and was crowned King Edward I as soon as he reached home.

Parliamentary Problems

During Edward's father's reign, the English barons had formed a Great Council – designed to keep an eye on the King. When Henry III resisted the Council, Simon de Montfort, the powerful Earl of Leicester, led a force against the King. Henry III was thrown into prison and the Earl seized power.

Earl Simon summoned all the great men of the realm and two knights and two citizens from every shire, to discuss the government of the kingdom. This is now known as the first English Parliament.

Henry's son, Edward, fought to avenge his imprisoned father and, in 1265, he defeated the barons, and Earl Simon was killed. Once Edward became king, however, he soon recognized that having a parliament would help him raise the money he needed to fund his battles abroad, so he allowed it to meet regularly.

In 1295, Edward summoned an even bigger council, consisting of barons, knights, important townspeople and members of the clergy, with the phrase 'let that which concerns everyone be approved by everyone'. This later became known as the Model Parliament, and is the distant relative of Britain's parliamentary system today. In fact, the word 'parliament' comes from the French word '*parler*' which means 'to talk'.

ROBERT THE BRUCE
1274 – 1329

Edward I was not content with only ruling England and, in 1296, he invaded Scotland and seized the throne for himself.

A Scot named William Wallace was less than pleased to have an English king on the Scottish throne, and gathered a group of rebels to fight off Edward. Wallace's rebels were joined by Robert the Bruce, a member of a powerful noble family in Scotland. After a series of bloody battles, Wallace was captured and hanged, drawn and quartered, but Robert was victorious and crowned himself king of Scotland, but he reigned only briefly before Edward I invaded again.

Defeated, but still determined to win, Robert the Bruce mounted repeated attacks on the English. When Edward I died, Robert seized his chance. He gathered an army of supporters and beat Edward's son, Edward II, at the Battle of Bannockburn in 1314. Robert was crowned king of Scotland again. In 1328, Scotland confirmed its independence from England.

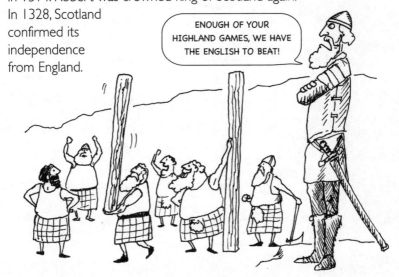

ENOUGH OF YOUR HIGHLAND GAMES, WE HAVE THE ENGLISH TO BEAT!

THE HUNDRED YEARS' WAR
1337 – 1453: Part One

Ever since William of Normandy had won the English throne at the Battle of Hastings in 1066, relations between the English and French kings had been very frosty.

Things took a turn for the worse in 1337, when Philip VI of France seized Gascony – an area of south-west France that had belonged to the kings of England for a long time. This fateful move triggered a period of fighting that lasted, on and off, for 116 years.

The Battle Of Crécy

King Edward III of England reacted to the French invasion by attacking land in northern France and claiming the French throne, which he believed was rightly his.

In 1346, at the Battle of Crécy, Philip fought Edward's invading army. His troops outnumbered Edward's, but the English army had a secret weapon – the longbow. Quicker to load and more deadly than the French crossbows, English longbows rained arrows down on the French cavalry. The English lost only about 40 men, but the French forces lost more than 1,500 knights.

Many more battles followed until, in 1360, the French surrendered some of their land to the English. A short period of peace followed, before fighting resumed and continued for years to come (see page 45).

THE BLACK DEATH
1348 – 1350

As if being worked to death on the land, being forced to pay high taxes, or being carted off to fight the French wasn't bad enough, in 1348 something even more terrible happened to the people of Britain – the Black Death.

Historians and scientists now think that the Black Death was a terrible plague caused by bacteria living in the bloodstream of rats. It was transferred to humans by fleas. To people living in Britain at the time, the arrival of the Black Death was a complete mystery. Some blamed the movement of the stars and planets; others believed that naughty children were to blame!

Plague Effects

In humans, the first sign of the disease would have been black, ugly swellings on the neck, armpits and groin – the colour of which gave the plague its name. Within a week, the plague's victims would be dead. A worse strain of the disease attacked the lungs and killed within 48 hours.

In an attempt to remove the poisons believed to be causing the illness, sufferers had blood drained from their veins and dried toads placed under their armpits. When entering the room of a sufferer, people were advised to pop cloves and two slices of bread soaked in wine into their mouths to stop the disease spreading. None of these cures worked, and it is estimated that more than a third of the population of England died.

43

POWER TO THE PEASANTS!
1381

The Black Death killed many people in Britain, and afterwards there were far fewer peasants to work on the land. As a result, the peasants began to demand higher wages for their services.

Things seemed to be looking up for the poor, but the rich soon decided enough was enough, and passed new laws to cut all peasants' wages. In an attempt to fund England's never-ending war against France, Parliament next introduced a poll tax (a tax that forced both rich and poor to pay the same amount of money to the government).

Revolting Peasants

In 1381, the peasants decided to revolt, and a craftsman named Wat Tyler led a huge crowd of them to London, where they ran riot and set fire to buildings. Tyler met King Richard II, who agreed to listen to the peasants' demands, but while the two men talked, the Lord Mayor of London drew a knife and stabbed Tyler. Wounded, Tyler escaped, but the King's men soon found him and chopped off his head.

All the rebel leaders were executed, but the revolt was considered a success because the poll taxes were later cancelled.

THE HUNDRED YEARS' WAR

1337 – 1453: Part Two

Remember the fighting between France and England at the end of Part One (see page 42)? Well, in 1415, Henry V of England stepped up the hostilities by invading France.

His army of about 12,000 men had not got far, however, when the soldiers suffered a bad case of dysentery (a disease that attacks the digestive system). With his men unable to fight because they needed the loo all day, Henry had no choice but to turn around and head home.

The Battle of Agincourt

As the morning mist cleared across the field of Agincourt on 25th October 1415, Henry spied a French army of about 40,000 men, including thousands of French knights, blocking his route home.

Henry ordered his archers to fire. The French knights refused to attack the English longbowmen because they believed there was more glory in killing English knights. As a result, they were slaughtered by a shower of arrows. Henry won a great victory.

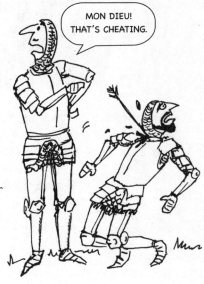

MON DIEU! THAT'S CHEATING.

Henry married the French King's daughter which brought peace for a while, but when Henry died soon afterwards, fighting started again. The French gradually reclaimed most of the land they had lost, until the English were defeated, and the Hundred Years' War finally came to an end.

THE WARS OF THE ROSES
1455 – 1485

In 1455, a civil war, known as the Wars of the Roses, broke out in England. It was a long and bloody struggle for the crown between two rival, powerful families, both of whom had a claim to the throne of England.

Rival Families

In the red corner was the House of Lancaster, whose symbol was a red rose. Henry VI, the king of England at the time, was a Lancastrian, but during his reign he suffered periods of insanity which made him unable to rule.

In the white corner was the House of York (and their symbol was a white rose). They were led by Richard, Duke of York, who was a cousin of Henry's.

Blood on Britain's Streets

Richard of York had already tasted power. In 1454, he had ruled the country while the King was too ill to govern. When King Henry recovered, Richard was suddenly totally excluded from power and decided to fight back.

The first battle of the Wars of the Roses was fought in the south of England in 1455. Richard was victorious, but the Lancastrians weren't completely beaten. They regrouped and, in 1460, fought back at the Battle of Wakefield in Yorkshire. Richard was killed and his severed head was displayed in the city of York for all to see.

But the Yorkists recovered from this grisly set-back, and Richard's son Edward managed to defeat the Lancastrians at the Battle of Towton in Yorkshire. The Yorkists threw Henry VI into the Tower of London, and crowned Edward king – King Edward IV of England.

The Kingmaker

Unfortunately, Edward IV soon fell out with his most powerful supporter – Richard Neville, the Earl of Warwick. Neville was also known as Warwick the Kingmaker for helping Edward to the throne, and he decided to 'make' another king. He rescued Henry VI from the Tower and put him back on the English throne in 1470.

Edward was not going to take this lying down, however. In 1471, he killed Neville and imprisoned Henry in the Tower again, where he was murdered. With his rivals safely out of the way, Edward ruled in relative calm until his death in 1483.

Edward IV was succeeded by his son, Edward V, who was, in turn, succeeded (and possibly murdered) by his uncle Richard III. The years of fighting finally ended in 1485, when Henry Tudor, a Lancastrian, was crowned Henry VII (see page 49).

RICHARD III AND
THE PRINCES IN THE TOWER

1452 – 1485 (Crowned 1483)

When Edward IV died, the heir to his throne was a 12-year-old boy, who became Edward V. Until he was old enough to rule, the young King's uncle Richard was asked to rule the country.

However, Richard proved the very opposite of a good uncle. He crowned himself Richard III, and kept Edward and his younger brother in the Tower of London. A month later, the two princes 'disappeared' – some people believe they were murdered on Richard's orders, though there is no real evidence of this.

As king, Richard III tried to introduce much-needed reforms, but he faced ongoing rebellions and the constant threat of invasion from France. This weakened his position, and a Lancastrian nobleman named Henry Tudor who had been living in France saw his chance and raised an army to fight Richard.

The rivals met in the middle of England at the Battle of Bosworth, Leicestershire, in 1485. Despite being outnumbered by Richard's soldiers, Henry's army was victorious. Richard was killed, and his body was stripped and paraded in public. One legend says his crown was found after the battle in a thorn bush, retrieved and placed on Henry's head.

The victorious Henry became Henry VII of England. He married Elizabeth of York, cleverly uniting the Houses of York and Lancaster. This marked the beginning of a new era in British history – the reign of the Tudor kings and queens.

Don't Believe All You Read ...

Did you know that William Shakespeare described Richard III in a play as a cruel man with a hunchback? As a result, most people think that this is what Richard III was really like.

In fact, historians believe that Richard was healthy and athletic and not a hunchback at all. Although, if the story is true, locking up and murdering your nephews is pretty cruel ...

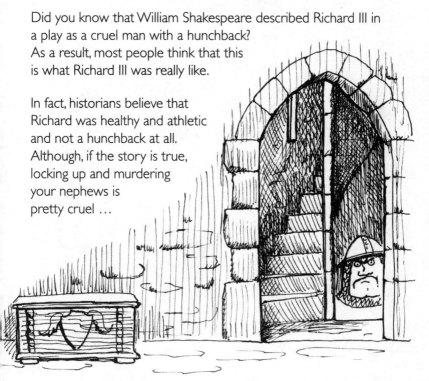

THE TUDORS

HENRY VIII

————— **1491 – 1547 (Crowned 1509)** —————

Henry VIII was never really supposed to be king. His older brother, Arthur, had been trained for the job, but he died unexpectedly. Young Henry became heir to the throne and was crowned king in 1509, after the death of his father Henry VII.

The new king was strong, athletic and reportedly very handsome. He loved poetry, music and dancing almost as much as he loved hunting and wrestling. He may even have composed a popular court hit called *Greensleeves*. Unfortunately though, he eventually became more famous for divorce than dancing.

Henry fought the French early in his reign, and found it a hard habit to shake. Among his fleet, a ship called the *Henri, Grâce à Dieu* was the world's biggest ship at the time and had 186 guns. Henry's reign saw many battles against France. In 1520, however, Henry met his rival, Francis I of France, at a sumptuous event called the Field of Cloth of Gold. Henry took the opportunity to show off his wealth and athleticism. It was said the two sides got on well, and that Henry and Francis even wrestled together but war continued.

Marital Madness

Henry's greatest problem at home was fathering a male heir. His first marriage to Catherine of Aragon (his elder brother's widow,) didn't produce a son, and he became determined to marry again. As a Catholic, however, Henry had to ask permission to end his marriage from the head of the Catholic Church – the Pope. When the Pope declined, Henry declared himself supreme head on earth of the Church in England. This move not only freed Henry to get rid of Catherine, but it also eventually led to the founding of the Church of England.

Free of the Pope's restraining powers, Henry turned his attention to looting Catholic monasteries throughout England. More than 800 were closed down, stripped of their riches and their land sold off. This made Henry much wealthier, but his destruction of the monasteries led to countless English treasures being lost or destroyed.

As time passed, Henry gradually turned against many of his most trusted friends and courtiers (the people who attended his royal court). He even beheaded one of his closest advisors, Sir Thomas More, for refusing to recognize his new power over the church. As his health declined, his temper grew worse, and eventually his love of food made him so grossly overweight he could not move without help.

IT'S TRUE, THE KING HAS GAINED A LITTLE WEIGHT SINCE THAT WAS PAINTED.

HENRY X

SIX WIVES FOR HENRY
1509 – 1547

Henry VIII married a grand total of six times. The dates below each of his wives' names show how long they stayed married to him. Read on to find out how one man got through so many women in one lifetime …

Catherine of Aragon
1509 – 1533

Catherine was married to Henry for more years than the rest of his wives put together. She gave birth to six children, including two sons, but they all died at birth or very young.
Only one child survived – Mary, who later became queen. Henry had his marriage to Catherine annulled, which means it was declared invalid.

Anne Boleyn
1533 – 1536

Henry's second wife, Anne Boleyn, gave birth to a baby girl who later became Queen Elizabeth I. But after Anne failed to produce a male heir, Henry accused her of having affairs with other men. She was put on trial and, when found guilty, she was beheaded at the Tower of London.

53

Jane Seymour
1536 – 1537

It seemed to be a case of third time lucky for Henry when he married Jane Seymour just two weeks after Anne Boleyn's execution. Jane gave birth to a boy who was to become King Edward VI. Sadly she died just 12 days after giving birth. It is thought that Jane was Henry's favourite wife, particularly because she bore him a son, and he was buried beside her.

Anne of Cleves
6th January 1540 – 9th July 1540

Henry's fourth marriage was arranged by one of his advisors, Thomas Cromwell. The marriage was designed to give Henry Protestant allies against the more powerful Catholic countries in Europe. Unfortunately, when he saw Anne, Henry described her as a 'Flanders Mare' (which was an old-fashioned way of saying she was ugly). Within six months the wedding was annulled. Cromwell paid for the failed marriage with his life, but Henry treated Anne fairly, giving her a generous income and several homes in England.

Catherine Howard
1540 – 1541

Still in her teens when she married Henry, poor Catherine was much younger than her 50-year-old husband. At first, Henry showered Catherine with gifts and affection. Catherine wasn't as keen on her fat, grumpy husband. On discovering his wife had had affairs with other men before their marriage, and perhaps after it too, Henry had her beheaded.

Catherine Parr
1543 – 1547

Henry's last wife was a religious, intellectual woman. Though her marriages didn't match Henry's total, Catherine had been wed and widowed twice before. She looked after Henry until he died in 1547, and was close to his children, Mary, Elizabeth and Edward.

Off With Whose Head?

A quick way of remembering how many of Henry's wives lost their heads is by learning this catchy little rhyme:

Divorced, beheaded, died,
Divorced, beheaded, survived.

LADY JANE GREY
1536/7 – 1554

When the sick, bloated Henry VIII died in 1547, the throne passed to his only son, Edward. King Edward VI was just nine years old at the time, and the country was ruled first by his uncle, the Duke of Somerset, and then by the Duke of Northumberland.

Determined to maintain and continue the changes Henry VIII had made to the official religion in England, both men wanted to prevent Mary Tudor (Henry VIII's eldest daughter and a Catholic) from coming to power. So, when Edward died aged only 15, the Duke of Northumberland quickly proclaimed his daughter-in-law Jane Grey (who was a Protestant) the new queen of England.

Queen for Nine Days

Said to be very beautiful and intelligent, 17-year-old Lady Jane Grey only survived nine days on the throne – the shortest reign in English history. Mary Tudor marched on London and claimed the throne for herself. After a short imprisonment in the Tower of London, Jane and her husband were beheaded. Mary did, however, grant her poor cousin the favour of being beheaded in private instead of in front of London's crowds … how kind!

MARY I
———— 1516 – 1558 (Crowned 1553) ————

Mary Tudor was crowned Mary I in 1553, and was the first,
fully fledged queen of England. But anyone expecting a gentle,
feminine touch was in for a shock.

As a committed Catholic, Mary set about persecuting Protestants
in the hope of bringing back Catholicism as the official religion in
England. She freed many Catholic priests who had been locked
up, and imprisoned many Protestant ones in their place. She even
married a Catholic, King Philip II of Spain, whom many of her
anti-Catholic subjects distrusted. They suspected that one day he
would want to control England himself – which he did (see pages
60 to 61).

Mary died in 1558, and her attempts to reunite England and the
Catholic Church died with her, because she didn't have an heir to
carry on her work.

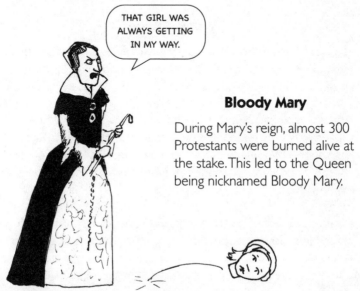

THAT GIRL WAS
ALWAYS GETTING
IN MY WAY.

Bloody Mary

During Mary's reign, almost 300
Protestants were burned alive at
the stake. This led to the Queen
being nicknamed Bloody Mary.

ELIZABETH I
—— 1533 – 1603 (Crowned 1558) ——

Henry VIII's daughter Elizabeth was crowned queen of England in 1558. She proved to be a successful, popular leader who, during her 45-year-long reign, helped England become a major world power.

Unlike her half-sister, Mary I, Elizabeth was a Protestant and during her reign she faced constant threats from her Catholic enemies. Several assassination attempts were made against her, but she survived them thanks to her very own spy network, set up by her trusted adviser, Sir Francis Walsingham.

It was one of Walsingham's spies who discovered evidence of a plot to assassinate Elizabeth and start a Catholic uprising. The plot involved her cousin, Mary Queen of Scots, who had been kept a prisoner by Elizabeth for 18 years. Faced with this evidence of her betrayal, Elizabeth reluctantly agreed to Mary's execution.

Women Rule!

In a world where power usually lay with kings and male courtiers, Elizabeth refused to marry. She claimed, 'I have already joined myself in marriage to a husband, namely the kingdom of England.'

Although she had several male favourites during her lifetime, the Queen was very good at keeping men in their place. Courtiers had to walk backwards out of her royal presence and, if anyone offended her, Elizabeth would threaten to 'make them shorter by a head'.

Elizabeth remained unmarried throughout her reign and had no children. So, when she died in 1603, the Tudor era came to an end.

Did You Know?

When Elizabeth died, 2,000 dresses were recorded in her wardrobe, and during her lifetime she was quite a fashion icon. Other ladies at court dyed their hair a similar shade of red to hers, while some even copied her decayed teeth by blacking out their own teeth with soot. Elizabeth was famous for her great cleanliness, and one source says she took four baths a year – whether she needed them or not!

THE SPANISH ARMADA
1588

In 1588, an enormous fleet of ships was spotted sailing over from Spain to invade England. Queen Elizabeth I was about to face the greatest threat to her rule … the Spanish Armada.

Seas of Treasure

In 1492, an explorer named Christopher Columbus had sailed to America and claimed it for Spain. Soon, hundreds of Spanish vessels, filled with treasures taken from the newly found lands, sailed the seas. All those ships laden with gold, silver and other valuable cargoes was just too tempting a prize for Queen Elizabeth to ignore.

She commissioned the seafarer Francis Drake to sail around the world and loot the treasure-filled Spanish ships in the Pacific Ocean. He brought back so much loot for Elizabeth that she made him a knight and an admiral in the English Navy.

Sir Francis' piracy soon upset King Philip II of Spain. He gathered a huge fleet (known in Spanish as an *armada*) and set off to invade England. The fleet consisted of 130 ships with about 8,000 seamen and as many as 19,000 soldiers.

In the nick of time, Elizabeth's spies discovered Philip's plans and prepared a counterattack. *El Draque*, as Drake was nicknamed by the Spanish (meaning the Dragon), conducted a surprise raid on the Armada resting in Cadiz at the southern tip of Spain. The Armada was left badly damaged.

Armada Attack

When the Armada had repaired its ships, it headed for England again. Beacons along the coast of Cornwall flared into life warning of its arrival. It was later reported that on hearing this news, Drake insisted on finishing his game of bowls before he prepared for battle, but nobody knows if this is true.

The English fleet was outnumbered by the Spanish, but the English ships were smaller, faster and well armed.

The English launched eight fire ships (ships that had been purposely set on

fire in the hope that they would set fire to enemy ships, too), which drifted towards the Spanish ships forcing them to scatter to avoid catching fire.

Bad weather and the English fleet's attack drove the Armada away. It was forced to sail around Britain and head home to Spain. Only 60 ships made it back and some 15,000 Spanish men lost their lives. The English fleet suffered hardly any losses in battle.

WILLIAM SHAKESPEARE
1564 – 1616

One person who lived during the Tudor period and is as famous as any king or queen, is a man named William Shakespeare. But despite his fame, and having written so many plays that are still performed today, little is known about the man himself.

Born in Stratford-upon-Avon, Shakespeare was sent to a grammar school. There he learnt to read and write English and Latin, and may have read texts by Classical Greek and Roman authors.

At 18, he married Anne Hathaway, and the couple had three children together. He started to write, and moved to London, where he worked for a theatre company. In his lifetime, Shakespeare wrote 154 sonnets (a sonnet is a special kind of poem that has 14 lines) and at least 38 plays. He even acted in some of his plays himself.

Shakespeare died on 23rd April 1616. Although by then he was a wealthy man, Shakespeare only left his wife his 'second-best bed' in his will! Engraved on his headstone was the warning below:

> Blest be the man that spares these stones,
> And curst be he that moves my bones.

So far, no one has dared risk the curse, and his grave remains undisturbed in Holy Trinity Church, Stratford-upon-Avon.

Did You Know?

Elizabethan audiences did not put up with poor performances, and people would throw things at the actors who weren't up to scratch. Women weren't allowed to act on the stage, so boys took female roles.

THE STUARTS

JAMES VI OF SCOTLAND
AND JAMES I OF ENGLAND

1566 –1625

(Crowned King of Scotland 1567)
(Crowned King of England 1603)

Queen Elizabeth died without any children, and so King James VI of Scotland (a member of the Stuart family and the son of Mary Queen of Scots) was crowned the king of England. The new Stuart King soon became very unpopular among his new subjects because he refused to participate in their English traditions.

James wasn't exactly a hunk either. In fact, one member of his court described James as having large eyes, a very thin beard and a tongue that was too large for his mouth. Despite his appearance, James had a very grand opinion of himself. He believed in the 'divine right of kings', which was the idea that God gave a king the power to rule. James refused to share his power with Parliament or anyone else.

The Stuart Schoolmaster

James liked to describe himself as the 'great schoolmaster of the whole land', and wanted to educate his subjects. He asked for a new translation of the Bible to be prepared that would be easier for people to read. James also hated tobacco smoking, which he described as a 'vile custom'. His constant preaching earned him the nickname the Wisest Fool in Christendom.

A group of extreme Protestants (called Puritans) strongly disapproved of the King's extravagant tastes and the way he boasted about his power. Some Puritans decided to leave England in protest. About 100 of them sailed to America to start a new life – they were later called the Pilgrim Fathers.

ACTUALLY YOUR MAJESTY, I BELIEVE IT'S MORE USUAL TO EAT THE POTATO AND SMOKE THE TOBACCO ...

James was determined to keep Protestantism the official religion of the country, and fought off any attempts to bring back Catholicism. This angered the Catholics, who wanted to be allowed to worship in peace. Constantly fearing assassination, James wore padded clothes to protect himself from being stabbed. Despite many attempts on his life – including a now famous plot to blow him up in 1605 (see page 66) – James lived to the ripe old age of 59 (which was quite old back then). After his death, his son inherited the throne and was crowned Charles 1.

Did You Know?

King James was the first king to use the term 'Great Britain'. He also created the Union Jack flag (a red, white and blue flag made out of the English and the Scottish flags). The British flag remained like this until 1801, when the Irish flag was added.

THE GUNPOWDER PLOT
5th November 1605

On the evening before the 5th November 1605, guards ran at breakneck speed through the cellars beneath the Palace of Westminster. With swords drawn, they peered down tunnels and into dark rooms. In the darkness, they spied a man, surrounded by barrels of gunpowder, waiting to light the fuse.

The guards' discovery foiled an ambitious plot to kill James I and blow up Parliament. The group who planned the assassination were Catholic extremists who desperately wanted a Catholic monarch on the throne. They managed to smuggle a man named

Guy Fawkes into the cellars with enough gunpowder to blow up the building. The explosion was planned for the next day, when the King and his family would be present to open Parliament.

Details of the plot were leaked just in time, and Fawkes was caught red-handed. He was tortured and hanged. His co-conspirators were found guilty of treason, hanged, and their bodies cut into pieces as a warning to others. Every year on the 5th November, bonfires are lit to remember the plot.

CHARLES I
1600 – 1649 (Crowned 1625)

When Charles inherited the throne from James I, he also inherited his father's belief in the divine right of kings (see page 64). Believing that his power came straight from God, he didn't want to listen to the advice of Parliament and, in 1629 he dismissed them and imprisoned some of its leaders. For the next 11 years, he ran the country without the aid of Parliament.

Cashless Charles

Without Parliament's powers, Charles struggled to raise enough money. He resorted to using ancient and unpopular methods of raising money. The most hated of these was a tax on coastal counties called 'ship money', which was used to help maintain the English Navy. Charles ordered that all counties in England had to pay ship money whether they had ports or not! The King even pawned many of the Crown Jewels to raise extra cash.

Charles tried to introduce a new prayer book in Scotland, which resulted in riots and the threat of war. The King had no choice but to recall Parliament and ask them for help.

Unsurprisingly, the Members of Parliament (MPs) had not forgotten how he had treated them, and insisted on making some changes. They set down all their complaints and tried to introduce laws to force the King to call Parliament. The King didn't like this one bit and, in 1642, he led soldiers into the House of Commons to arrest his critics.

Charles' raid failed because the MPs were forewarned and had time to escape capture. They retreated to raise an army and fight back. England was about to be plunged into civil war.

Civil War

The English Civil War was fought between the Royalists, the followers of Charles I, who were also named Cavaliers and wore their hair long like the King, and the Parliamentarians, also named Roundheads because they cut their hair short around their ears and wore round helmets.

The war that followed would split friends, families and the country down the middle. Charles' supporters included people in the north, the west and in Wales, while people in the south-east sided with Parliament. With more money and the ability to move equipment around the country, the Parliamentarians had the advantage over the Royalists.

Oliver Cromwell's New Model Army

Charles kicked off the fighting when he marched the Royal Army (based in Nottingham) to London to recapture the city from the Parliamentarians. The first few battles slowed down the King's advance, but it wasn't until an MP named Oliver Cromwell created an army made up of professional soldiers (called the New Model Army), that the Parliamentarians had a decisive victory.

At the Battle of Naseby in 1645, Cromwell's army finally defeated the badly organized Royalists. Charles asked the Scots to protect him, which they did briefly, but then handed him to Parliament. A second war broke out when, from his prison cell, the King persuaded the Scots to switch sides, and they briefly joined the Royalists to fight Parliament. But eventually the Royalists were defeated again and Charles was beheaded in 1649.

Cromwell abolished the monarchy and was made Lord Protector in 1653. Cromwell ruthlessly put down rebellions across the country and enforced strict, religious values. He closed down inns and playhouses, and even banned feasting on Christmas Day. After his death, his son Richard stepped into his shoes – but not for long!

THE MONARCHY RETURNS
1660 – 1685

Richard Cromwell was not as tough and ruthless as his father Oliver. The army grew sick of his strict laws and invited Charles I's eldest son to become king. He was crowned Charles II.

Charles II had survived the English Civil War by escaping to Europe. Legend says he disguised himself as a woodsman and hid in the branches of an old oak tree while the Parliamentarians searched the ground below.

Charles' acceptance of the throne marked the beginning of a period known as the Restoration – when power was restored to the monarchy.

A Very Merry Monarch

As king, Charles quickly got rid of the strict religious laws enforced by Cromwell. He was a handsome, fun-loving king who enjoyed a 'mad range of pleasure', including gambling and horse racing. He re-opened theatres and pubs and was soon nicknamed the Merry Monarch. England had become a rich country and was beginning to colonize territories abroad and increase trade around the world. The rich showed off their wealth by building grand houses, and a new craze swept the country with the arrival of an exotic new drink – coffee. Sadly, it wasn't to be long before disaster struck.

69

STRUCK BY PLAGUE AND FIRE
1665 – 1666

During the reign of King Charles II, London had become a thriving city. The streets, however, grew increasingly filthy and crowded – ideal conditions for diseases to spread.

Sure enough, in 1665, a terrible plague erupted in the city. Just like in the Black Death of 1348 (see page 43), the Bubonic plague of 1665 was spread to humans by fleas living on infected rats.

BEFORE ...

To try to stop the death toll rising, London's locals took desperate measures. Victims were locked in their houses and a cross was marked on the doors to warn people not to enter. Cats and dogs were rounded up and slaughtered, in an attempt to kill the disease-carrying fleas that lived on them. Unfortunately, all this did was wipe out the animals that killed the rats, so the rats bred faster. Around a fifth of the entire population of London died from the plague.

But London's suffering was not over yet. In the hot summer in 1666, a huge fire gripped the city. It started in a small bakery on Pudding Lane, near London Bridge. Fanned by a strong easterly wind, the flames rapidly devoured London's tightly packed wooden buildings, raging from street to street. With no fire brigade to help them, the city's inhabitants battled the flames for four days, pulling down the buildings in their path to stop the fire spreading.

... AFTER

By the time the fire was out, it had destroyed more than 13,000 houses in an area roughly one and a half square kilometres in size, though few people actually died. The Great Fire of London, as it became known, did have some benefits though. It killed the rats and fleas that had spread the plague, and a new architect named Christopher Wren was hired to re-design London. Unfortunately, money ran out and Wren and his team were only able to build a few famous landmarks seen in London today, including the impressive St Paul's Cathedral.

THE GLORIOUS REVOLUTION
——————— 1688 ———————

When Charles II died in 1685, his brother James inherited the throne. To the disappointment of many Protestants in England, however, James II was a faithful Catholic.

The Protestants hoped that James, at 51 years old, was too old to produce a male heir, and were willing to wait for the throne to pass to his Protestant daughter, Mary. Unfortunately, the arrival of the King's healthy newborn son ruined this plan.

The Protestants turned to Plan B. They invited James' daughter, Mary, and her Dutch husband, a Protestant prince named William of Orange, to come and overthrow James. In an event known as the Glorious Revolution, the couple invaded England. King James II fled to France, throwing the Great Seal (used to stamp Royal documents) into the River Thames as he left.

William III and Mary II were jointly crowned king and queen of England in 1689. Soon after, Parliament voted to limit the power of future monarchs and stated they had to be Protestant. Catholics were barred from the throne.

In less than a year, James returned with an army, but he was defeated at the Battle of the Boyne, in Ireland. When Mary and William died, the throne passed to Mary's sister, Anne. Anne died without a surviving heir, despite having given birth to 19 children.

Did You Know?

King William III died in 1702 from the injuries he suffered after his horse stumbled on a molehill, throwing him to the ground. Supporters of the Stuart king, James II, often raised a glass to toast the 'little gentleman in black velvet' (the mole) who had caused the death of their enemy.

GEORGIAN BRITAIN

MEET THE GEORGES
1714 – 1830

The coronation of George I marked the start of the Georgian era – a period in which four Protestant kings ruled Britain, and each was named George.

George I (Reigned 1714 – 1727)

George I came from Germany and didn't speak much English. While he spent much of his reign in his homeland, he did manage to crush attempts by rebellious supporters of the Stuarts (known as Jacobites) to put Queen Anne's half-brother, James Stuart, back on the throne of Scotland.

George II (Reigned 1727 – 1760)

When George I died, no one in Britain was very sad, least of all his son George, who inherited the throne. George had hated his father ever since he imprisoned his mother for having an affair. During George II's reign, the Jacobites were beaten at the Battle of Culloden Moor, and the last Stuart claimant to the throne, a man known as Bonnie Prince Charlie, was sent packing.

George III (Reigned 1760 – 1820)

George III was George II's grandson (his father had died when he was 12), but unlike the Georges before him, he was a big fan of Britain. His love of science and his interest in the arts helped to bring 'the Enlightenment' to Britain from Europe (this was a movement that believed in the power of learning). Tragically, George suffered from bouts of insanity, so his son (also named George) was made Prince Regent and ruled on his behalf.

During George's reign, the British Empire grew and grew, but America, in contrast, gained its independence from Britain.

Colonists living in America resented British rule and paying high taxes so, in 1773, they staged a dramatic protest. Disguised as Native Americans wearing feathered headdresses and face paint, protestors stormed on board a trading ship. They threw overboard 342 chests of tea – an expensive cargo, which was heavily taxed.

The rebels' actions that day became known as the Boston Tea Party, and it set the ball rolling for American independence. George III sent the British Army to fight the rebels, but after years of fighting the British were finally beaten at the Battle of Yorktown in 1781. Two years later the United States of America was created.

George IV (Reigned 1820 – 1830)

When his father died, the Prince Regent was crowned George IV. The new King preferred spending time with his mistresses rather than his wife – he didn't even invite her to his coronation! Despite being a lover of the arts and founding the British Library (to which he donated all his father's books), he died in debt and unloved by his subjects.

THE INDUSTRIAL REVOLUTION
Around 1750 – 1830

The Industrial Revolution is the name given to a period that saw a series of dramatic changes in farming, trade and manufacturing in Britain that would alter people's lives forever.

It all kicked off with major changes in farming methods. As new, efficient machinery was introduced, fewer farm labourers were needed to work the land. People began to move to the cities to find work in the new factories that were being built. Whereas before most people lived in the countryside, now the population of towns and cities began to grow.

Industrious Inventions

Meanwhile, new tools, machines and manufacturing techniques were being invented. A Scottish engineer named James Watt developed a steam engine so efficient it had the power to run a whole factory. This meant that goods could now be made quickly and cheaply. By 1800, more than 500 of Watt's engines were being used to power Britain's factories. The watt (the term used to describe a unit of power today) is named after James.

Steam engines were also used to power the railways that were built throughout Britain to transport the goods being made in

I WISH I LIVED IN THE CITY ...

the factories across the country. Britain's roads were also improved, which cut down the time it took to get around.

A man named Richard Arkwright revolutionized the cloth-making industry with his invention of a mechanically powered spinning wheel. From 1771, water wheels were used to power the machine, and production of cloth doubled. Britain found itself getting steadily richer.

Fuming Factory Workers

As more new equipment and methods were introduced to factories throughout the country, workers began to lose their jobs as their work could be performed more efficiently by machines. In 1811, workers destroyed two new machines in a textile factory in protest. These 'Luddite' protests (as they became known) spread. Factory owners called in the army and some protesters were shipped off to work in newly discovered Australia – which was established as Britain's prison colony.

BRITANNIA RULES THE WAVES
mid-1700s

Throughout the seventeenth and eighteenth centuries, hundreds of ships set sail from British ports hoping to claim new lands and trade routes for Britain. They returned home laden with cotton and tobacco from North America, sugar and rum from the Caribbean and South America, and tea and silk from India and China.

Companies were set up to trade these treasures with other countries, and Britain soon became one of the richest countries in the world. British trading companies went about seizing land and resources worldwide. The lands Britain ruled, known as the British Empire, grew and grew. It wasn't all plain sailing though – other European countries were doing the same thing. Soon fighting broke out over who owned what.

Bagsy That Bit!

The Americas became the battleground for the British against their French rivals. The French had already conquered areas in Canada, but the British wanted all of it for themselves. In 1759, the British performed a surprise attack on the French headquarters at Québec in Canada led by the British General James Wolfe. The city was captured and the French surrendered their lands to Britain.

Further south, the Brits weren't so lucky. Many people living in the American colonies wanted to rule themselves. In 1776, 13 colonies declared their independence from British rule. The British fought to resist, but by 1783 they had to admit defeat.

Losing their American lands was a serious blow to Britain's pride, but it didn't stop her Empire growing. By the 1760s, the (British) East India Company, a trading company so large and powerful it had its own army, was in control of most of the Indian continent.

British explorers were busy sailing the seas. Over the course of several voyages, an explorer named Captain James Cook sailed to New Zealand, Australia, the Antarctic and numerous islands in the Pacific.

In Africa, the Scottish explorer James Bruce went to what was then believed to be the source of the longest river in the world, the Nile. A Scot, named Mungo Park, travelled up the Niger River in central Africa. Voyages such as these made Britain much more aware of the rich opportunities that the wider world offered.

By the 1870s, Britain had established colonies throughout the world. It was popular to boast at the time that 'the sun never sets on the British Empire' – this means the Empire was so vast that, no matter what time of day or night it was in Britain, there was always daylight somewhere in the British Empire.

PIRATES OF THE CARIBBEAN
1700s

A life on the ocean waves was definitely not an easy one for sailors. Sudden storms and hidden reefs could rip their boats to shreds, but their greatest fear was another danger that stalked the high seas – pirates.

Some pirates worked for the governments of different countries. Known as privateers, their job was to attack enemy ships and take their cargoes. Privateers would keep part of their loot and give the rest to the government that they worked for.

Pirating Pranks

Pirates weren't exactly known for their good behaviour. There was one particularly bloodthirsty pirate named Edward Teach – otherwise known as Blackbeard (unsurprisingly, because of his black beard). He started his career working for the British government, but later began stealing for himself. He went about raiding ships and land around the Caribbean Sea. His scary habits are said to have included cutting fingers off his victims to take their rings, shooting at his own crew, and putting smoking cannon fuses in his hair before going in to battle.

Eventually, Blackbeard was hunted down by a British naval force. Some said it took five bullets and 20 sword thrusts to kill him. The pirate's head was cut off, and it was hung from the front of a British ship as a warning to others.

Did You Know?

Despite what you see in films, ropes, sails and medical supplies were just as valuable to pirate crews as gold and jewels. Also, there isn't any evidence that pirates made their victims walk the plank.

NELSON'S BATTLE AT TRAFALGAR
21ˢᵗ October 1805

The French Revolution began in 1789. It was a bloody revolt during which the heads of the French monarchy and thousands of aristocrats were removed. Chaos reigned, until Napoleon, a French general, seized power. He made himself Emperor of France, and set out to expand French power across Europe. Britain fought to stop him.

On a cold, grey morning on 21ˢᵗ October 1805, west of Cape Trafalgar, Spain, a British admiral named Horatio Nelson stood on the deck of the HMS *Victory*. He was a brilliant man. At just 20 years old, he had been put in charge of sea defence against Napoleon. He had already fought the Spanish, and in battle lost his right arm and the sight in his right eye. Now he spied the ships of the French Navy forming a single line ready to attack. He gave an order to his crew, 'England expects that every man will do his duty.'

Tactics at Trafalgar

The Battle of Trafalgar was Nelson's finest victory. He ordered his 27 ships to form two squadrons and attack the line of French ships at right angles,

ONE EYE, ONE ARM AND NO SEA LEGS. WHAT USE IS HE?

81

'like a spear'. It was a high-risk plan, but Nelson believed it would work. And it did. The French fleet were scattered across the sea. The British captured 19 or 20 French ships, and 14,000 of their sailors. French naval powers never recovered from this defeat.

Nelson didn't live to see his victory. A French sniper's bullet pierced his chest and shoulder. It is said his last words were, 'Now I am satisfied. Thank God, I have done my duty.' Nelson's body was pickled in a barrel of brandy and taken back to England where he was buried in St Paul's Cathedral, after a grand funeral.

AN END TO THE SLAVE TRADE
25th March 1807

Since the sixteenth century, Britain had been making huge sums of money from the slave trade. It was a booming business that transported more than ten million African people on ships to the Americas, where they were sold as slaves. British cities such as Bristol, Liverpool and London grew rich on the proceeds.

Conditions on board slave ships were horrific. More than a third of the hundreds of people crammed aboard each ship died from disease or thirst. Some threw themselves overboard to escape the unbearable conditions. In 1789, a Nigerian ex-slave named Olaudah Equino wrote about his experiences. He described a slave captain who threw 133 chained slaves overboard, then claimed money for losses on his insurance policy! Stories such as these began to turn public opinion in Britain against the trade.

A Member of Parliament named William Wilberforce made a speech against the trade. The House of Commons voted in favour of the abolition of slavery in 1807, but it took another 30 years for the trade to stop completely throughout the British Empire.

WELLINGTON AND WATERLOO
18th June 1815

Napoleon successfully conquered many countries, but eventually his luck ran out. A disastrous campaign in Russia forced him to give up his title. He was exiled from France briefly, but returned in 1815 to raise an army. Napoleon had an ambitious plan – to march on Belgium.

Time for the Boot

Desperate to stop Napoleon building up his empire again, the British and their European friends gathered two armies.

Arthur Wellesley, the first Duke of Wellington, commanded the British-Dutch army, while Count Von Blücher led a larger force from the German state of Prussia (in modern northern Germany).

> I'M NOT TALKING ABOUT YOUR BOOTS WELLINGTON, I SAID IT'S TIME WE GAVE THAT NAPOLEON THE BOOT!

The Battle of Waterloo

Wellington's and Blücher's armies set off separately to march through Belgium to meet Napoleon's forces. Napoleon knew that he would not be able to defeat both armies, so, in a desperate attempt to gain the upper hand, he launched a lightning attack on Blücher's army. The Prussians were forced to retreat but three days later, on 18th June 1815, Napoleon met Wellington's army, near the town of Waterloo, just south of Brussels.

Napoleon launched the first attack, but the British held their ground. By early evening both armies had fought themselves to a standstill. Then the Prussian army appeared. Wellington and Blücher sent new, fresh men into the battle. Napoleon's men were too tired to fight back, and were forced to retreat. Napoleon's army suffered huge losses, with 25,000 men killed or wounded and 9,000 captured. Wellington's army suffered 15,000 casualties and Blücher's about 8,000. Napoleon was banished to Saint Helena Island in the South Atlantic, where he died. Some people believe he was poisoned.

Wellington returned to Britain a hero. He described his victory against Napoleon as a 'damned near-run thing'. He became Prime Minister in 1828, and was given a majestic state funeral after his death, in honour of his achievements.

Did You Know?

One day, Wellington asked his shoemaker to make him a boot that was strong enough for battle, but comfortable enough to wear out to dinner. His bootmaker did a fine job, and the new style of boots became all the rage among the British officers. When told that the ship he was sailing in might be wrecked, Wellington reportedly exclaimed, 'In that case, I won't take off my boots!' This is why we call waterproof boots 'Wellington' boots.

VICTORIAN BRITAIN

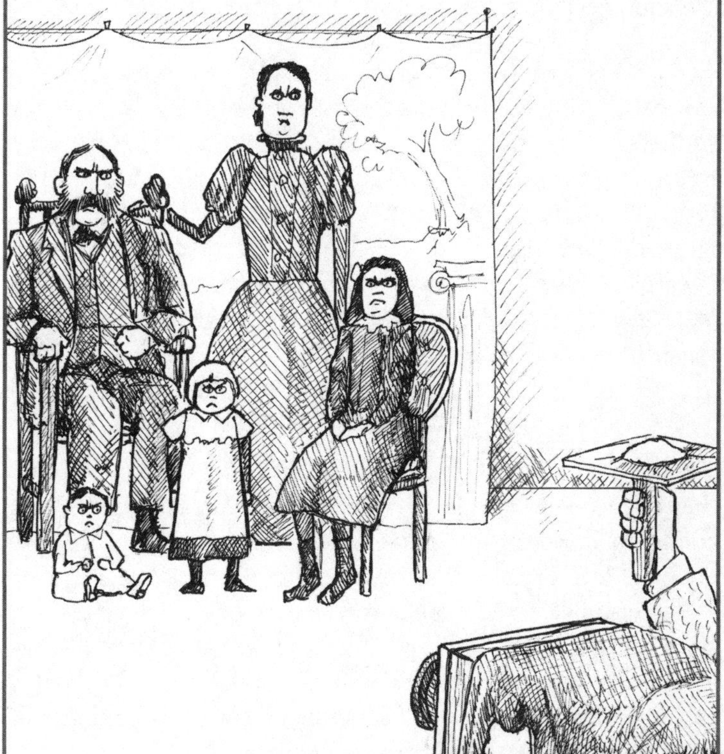

QUEEN VICTORIA
1819 – 1901 (Crowned 1838)

Queen Victoria is often remembered as a stern, old woman dressed in black. However, she wasn't always like that. In fact, Victoria was just 18 years old when she became queen, and she soon became the most powerful monarch on the planet.

Her reign got off to a very grand start with a magnificent coronation. At the time, Britain's trade and industry were thriving and, with a new young monarch on the throne, the people of Britain felt very positive about the future. In many ways, Victoria's reign did not disappoint them. Britain's Empire expanded, and huge advances were made in healthcare, education and science. It wasn't all rosy, though, as Victorian Britain was at war in Africa, battling to control uprisings in Ireland, and more than a third of the British people lived in poverty.

The Best of British

Victoria married her German cousin, Prince Albert, in 1840, and they had nine children. During his lifetime, Albert helped Victoria considerably. He organized the Great Exhibition (an event designed to show off riches – both those produced by British industry and gathered from around the Empire). The exhibits were housed in a beautiful glass building called the Crystal Palace in Hyde Park, London. Around six million people came to marvel at the wonders on display, which included cutting-edge designs of household objects and treasures from around the world.

Unfortunately, there was no 'happily ever after' for the royal couple. Albert died in 1861 from typhoid (a disease caught from drinking dirty water). Victoria went into mourning, wearing black widow's clothes for the rest of her life. She even stopped going out in public. As a result, her popularity dipped until the Prime

Minister at that time, Benjamin Disraeli, persuaded the Queen to reappear in public. Victoria's golden and diamond jubilees (50 and 60 year anniversaries of being queen) were huge celebrations. She never forgot Albert though, and built the Royal Albert Hall as a tribute to him.

Her own death, aged 81, marked the longest reign of any British monarch so far. Millions of people attended her funeral.

Did You Know?

Prince Albert introduced to Britain the traditions of decorating Christmas trees and sending Christmas cards.

WELL, I NEVER, A BREAKFAST EGG BOILER!

DON'T WE HAVE SERVANTS FOR THAT?

87

VICTORIAN PIONEERS
19th century

Victorian Britons saw an explosion of new ideas and inventions. Every day, pioneers in science, engineering and the arts were busy creating new things.

Sir Robert Peel
1788 – 1850

Peel worked to establish the first trained police force. Its officers were nicknamed 'Bobby's boys' or 'Peelers' after him, and policeman are still known as 'bobbies' today.

Robert Stephenson
1803 – 1859

Stephenson was a brilliant civil engineer who helped to power the train revolution in Britain. He built many tracks and bridges across the country, and designed a hugely improved engine.

Isambard Kingdom Brunel
1806 – 1859

At just 24 years old, Brunel won a competition to design the Clifton Suspension Bridge. He went on to design tunnels, docks and bridges, and the world's biggest steam-powered passenger ship called the SS *Great Britain*.

Sir Richard Owen
1804 – 1892

After studying fossils that he had found, Owen named the giant creatures that had formed them *dinosauria* (which means 'terrible lizard' in Greek). Owen developed the Natural History Museum in London where his fossils are displayed.

Charles Dickens
1812 – 1870

Dickens wrote gripping stories and set many of them in Victorian London. His novel *The Pickwick Papers* (1837) made him the most popular English novelist of his time.

Joseph Lister
1827 – 1912

Hospitals in Victorian Britain were filthy places until Lister introduced the use of antiseptics. Far fewer people died in Britain's hospitals as a result.

Joseph Bazalgette
1819 – 1891

Bazalgette solved the stinky problem of London sewage by designing a system of underground tunnels to take waste away from the city. This cut down disease and made the city smell sweeter.

IRISH POTATO FAMINE
1845 – 1851

Sometimes the smallest thing can have a huge impact on history, and things don't come much smaller than *Phytophthora infestans*. That's the scientific name for a fungus that infected Ireland's potato crops in 1845. The blight (the name used to refer to the disease) and wet weather turned Ireland's potato crops into an inedible, stinking slime in 1845 and again in 1846.

Ireland had been part of the United Kingdom since 1801. Most of its land was owned by wealthy Englishmen. Rather than helping the Irish tenants who could not pay their rent because potato crops had failed, some landlords cruelly threw them off the land. One and a half million people died of disease and starvation.

The Irish people turned against England, and later, in the 1880s, a politician named Charles Parnell campaigned for Ireland to rule itself. He organized rent strikes and protests. The quarrel over Ireland's independence would rage for many years to come.

CASUALTIES IN CRIMEA
1854 – 1856

The Crimean War was a series of battles fought to stop Russia expanding its territory in the Crimea (now Ukraine). One battle was described by a French general as 'magnificent, but it isn't war – it's stupidity.' Stupid sums up the war pretty well. The armies sent to the Crimea by Britain, France and Turkey were so poorly equipped and badly led, that the consequences were disastrous.

At the Battle of Balaklava on 25th October 1854, a confused order resulted in a British cavalry unit called the Light Brigade charging directly at Russian guns. More than a third of the 673 men that charged were killed or wounded. The English poet Alfred Lord Tennyson described the bravery of the men in these lines from his famous poem *The Charge of the Light Brigade*:

> Stormed at with shot and shell,
> Boldly they rode and well,
> Into the jaws of Death,
> Into the mouth of Hell,
> Rode the six hundred.

Lady of the Lamp

The battles were chaotic and bloody, but the conditions in the hospitals were even worse. Injured soldiers were left on floors and subjected to grisly operations. The death toll was huge.

The Crimean War was the first to have newspaper reporters on the front line. When a woman named Florence Nightingale saw their reports, she was shocked. She managed to persuade the army to allow her to take 38 nurses to the Crimea.

Known as the Lady of the Lamp because of her frequent night visits on wards, Florence cleaned up the hospitals and cut the number of deaths. When the war ended she returned to England, and founded the Nightingale School of Nursing.

I CAN SEE YOU'VE STOLEN MY LAMP, YOU KNOW!

MUTINY IN INDIA
May 1857 – March 1858

In far-off India, a seemingly small thing happened that would change history forever.

The Honourable East India Company – a British trading company – had been governing India since the 1600s. It even had its own private army. When a story spread that its 'sepoys' (Indian soldiers under British command) had been issued with bullets coated with animal fat, trouble exploded. The use of animal fat was very insulting to the sepoys' religious beliefs, and they refused to use them. Mutinies (which means revolts) spread. British troops fought to restore order, and both sides carried out terrible massacres before the mutiny was suppressed.

After the mutiny, the British government decided the only way to restore their power throughout India was to take over the whole continent. So they did. India became a huge source of wealth for the Empire, and Queen Victoria was given the title Empress of India.

CHARLES DARWIN
1809 – 1882

In 1831, a British naval ship called the HMS Beagle set sail from England on a five-year expedition. On board was a 22-year-old naturalist (a person who studies nature) named Charles Darwin. Despite suffering from terrible seasickness, Darwin spent the trip collecting plants, wildlife, fossils and rocks. The ship visited many places in the southern hemisphere, including South America and Australia, and Darwin returned home with thousands of specimens – including a giant turtle from the Galapagos Islands.

After studying his specimens, Darwin noticed that finches (a type of bird) from different islands varied in size and shape. He concluded that species of plants and animals evolved (which means developed) to suit their environment, and they then passed down these characteristics.

In 1859, Darwin published *On the Origin of Species by Means of Natural Selection*. In this work, he argued that creatures and plants evolved over time. Most Victorians were outraged because they believed that God created the world and everything in it in seven days. His theory upset religious people across the globe, but is now internationally recognized.

EDUCATION FOR EVERYONE
1870

The next time you have an awful exam, you'll know who to blame – the Victorians. In 1870, an MP named William Forster introduced the Elementary Education Act to Parliament. This made education free (and compulsory) for children up to the age of 12.

Before this, one third of British people couldn't read or write. Only rich children could afford to go to school, and poor children were usually sent to do dirty, dangerous jobs, such as sweeping chimneys or working in cotton mills.

Painful Punishments

School in Victorian times was no holiday camp though. Teachers often had huge classes of up to 70 children, and pupils had to learn lessons by heart. Discipline was harsh, with many children beaten for talking or making tiny mistakes. Punishments suffered by Victorian school children included being struck with a cane, being locked in a wooden frame called the stocks, or even put in a basket that was hung from the ceiling!

THE SCRAMBLE FOR AFRICA

1879 – 1902

At the beginning of the 1870s, only about 10% of Africa was controlled by European countries, including France, Britain and Portugal. Yet by 1900, Europeans ruled over 90% of the continent. The competition between European nations for territory in Africa became known as the Scramble for Africa.

Britain started colonizing parts of Africa without too much difficulty. Victorian Britons moved there, building churches, schools and hospitals. However, in some areas they met resistance. When the British faced a Zulu tribe in the south of Africa, at the Battle of Isandhlwana in 1879, the British were defeated despite their guns, by men using only spears and shields.

Fighting the Boers

The British fought for the land in southern Africa against the Dutch settlers, called the Boers, who already lived there. In one battle during the First Boer War, a specially trained group of Boer fighters called commandos killed 93 British soldiers, yet suffered only one fatality themselves.

When gold and diamonds were found in southern Africa, the fighting began again. The British Commander, Lord Kitchener, ordered his soldiers to destroy Boer farms and imprison the families in camps, where thousands died. Eventually the Boers surrendered and the land became part of Britain's Empire.

Did You Know?

A Scottish missionary (a member of a religious expedition), David Livingstone, was the first European to see the huge waterfalls on the Zambezi River in 1855. He named them Victoria Falls after Queen Victoria.

EDWARDIAN BRITAIN

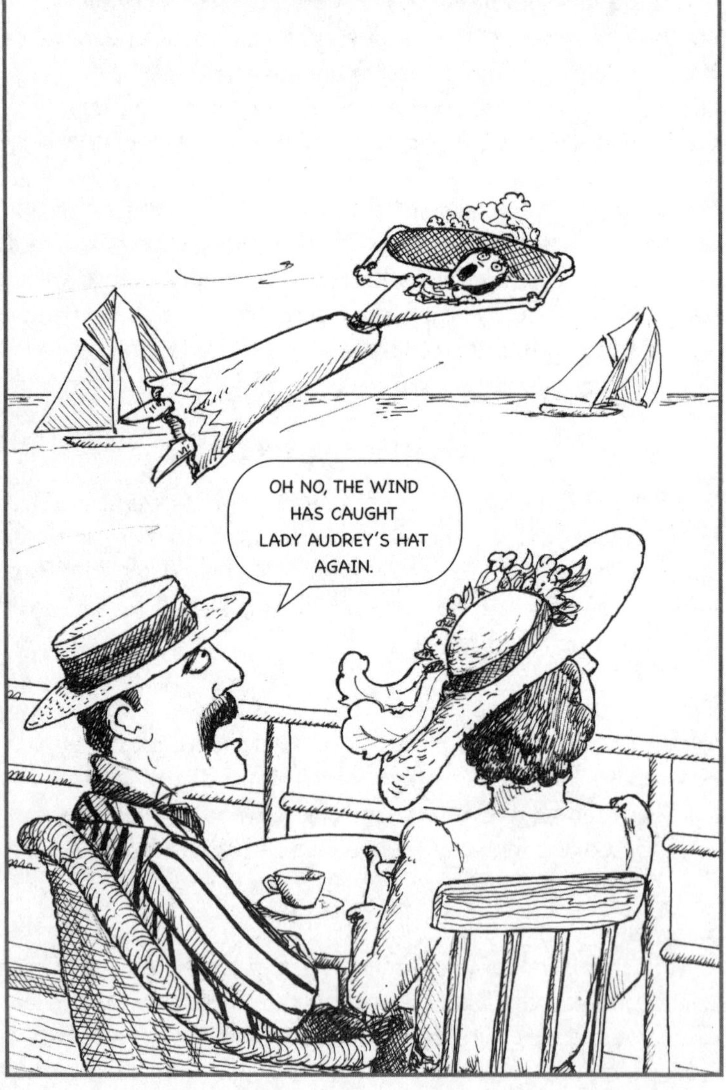

GETTING THE VOTE
1928

When Queen Victoria died in 1901, her son inherited the throne. Edward VII, the stylish new king, loved anything fast and modern – including horse racing, fast cars and fine dining. His attitude reflected the hope and optimism the country felt at the beginning of a new century.

There was one area, however, where Britain was still very traditional. Despite Queen Victoria having been one of the most powerful rulers in the world, she described the idea of women being allowed to vote in matters of state as 'mad, wicked folly'. Indeed Edwardian women weren't treated as men's equals in society. Up until 1882, wives were regarded as their husband's possessions and their only job was to look after the home.

Things started changing in 1897, when campaigners for suffrage (which means the right to vote) formed the National Union of Women's Suffrage Societies (NUWSS). Its members held political rallies and gathered petitions with the aim of winning women the vote. In 1903, however, a woman named Emmeline Pankhurst decided to take matters into her own hands.

Society Shockers

Pankhurst started a group whose members became known as suffragettes. The group's call for action was, 'Deeds not words.' Its members certainly lived up to this promise by carrying out acts that shocked society. At a time when displaying an ankle was seen as rather naughty and wearing trousers was scandalous, women kicked off their campaign by organizing large demonstrations in central London.

When the MPs still refused to listen to their requests, suffragettes started throwing stones through MPs' windows. They chained themselves to the railings outside 10 Downing St., home of the Prime Minister. When MPs still didn't listen, they burnt down churches and invaded clubs that only allowed in male members.

The authorities arrested many suffragettes, but some responded by going on hunger strike. When reports reached the suffragettes that the prisoners were being force-fed, they were outraged. One member of the group, Emily Davison, protested by throwing herself under a horse that belonged to the King at the Epsom Derby in 1913 – she died.

The suffragettes continued to campaign, but Pankhurst called a halt to activities when the First World War began. While some voting rights were granted in 1918, all women were given the vote in 1928.

THE SINKING OF THE *TITANIC*
14th / 15th April 1912

High above the calm sea in the crow's nest of RMS *Titanic*, a sailor rubbed his tired eyes. Midnight was approaching as he scrutinized the horizon. Suddenly, a huge grey shape caught his gaze and his heart began to race as he sounded the alarm – there was an iceberg and it was dead ahead …

When the *Titanic* set sail on its maiden (first ever) voyage on 10th April 1912, it was the largest passenger ship in the world. Built in Belfast, Northern Ireland, it set new standards in luxury. It had a gym, a library, beautiful large banqueting rooms and a vast ballroom. The liner was carrying more than 2,000 passengers – ranging from some of the world's richest people on a pleasure cruise, to poor people bound for a new life in America.

ICEBERG DEAD AHEAD!

The ship was only four days into its voyage, when the iceberg was spotted. She collided with it. At first, the impact didn't seem major – it was described as like the 'tearing of calico' (which is a type of cloth). But the collision made a hole in the *Titanic* below the waterline. It took less than three hours for the enormous vessel to fill with water and vanish beneath the icy waves. Too few lifeboats, freezing temperatures, and the fact that only one ship, the RMS *Carpathia*, came to the *Titanic's* rescue, meant that 1,517 people perished.

The ship that had famously been described as 'unsinkable' proved to be only too sinkable.

THE FIRST WORLD WAR YEARS

THE FIRST WORLD WAR
1914 – 1918

On 28th June 1914, in the Bosnian city of Sarajevo, a Bosnian Serb named Gavrilo Princip pulled a revolver from his pocket and shot dead Archduke Franz Ferdinand. The Archduke was heir to the Austro-Hungarian throne, and his assassination triggered a chain of events that plunged Europe into war.

Taking Sides

Since the nineteenth century, Germany had been building up its Navy hoping to expand its empire. This angered Britain who had always prided itself in having the biggest Navy in Europe. Worried that a war would break out, the rest of Europe started splitting into two rival sides. Austria-Hungary, Germany and the Ottoman Empire stuck together on one side and on the other, Britain, France and Russia became the 'Allies' (meaning they would fight together).

The assassination of the Archduke was all it took to start a world war. Austria-Hungary quickly declared war on Serbia. Both Russia and France rushed to Serbia's defence, and Germany seized the opportunity it had been waiting for and sided with Austria-Hungary. Then, on 4th August 1914, Germany invaded Belgium on its way to attack France. Britain rushed to protect them. The First World War had begun.

The Battle Through Europe

The German army got within about 50 kilometres of Paris before they were halted at the River Marne by British and French troops. The Germans dug ditches called trenches, and the French and British forces did the same. Both armies faced each other along a line of trenches hundreds of kilometres long, known as the Western Front. Two million men from Britain volunteered to fight, but thousands died, as generals on both sides ordered wave after

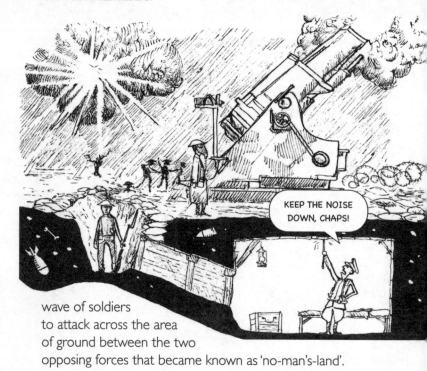

KEEP THE NOISE
DOWN, CHAPS!

wave of soldiers
to attack across the area
of ground between the two
opposing forces that became known as 'no-man's-land'.

On 1st July 1916, the Battle of the Somme began, in which 420,000 British soldiers lost their lives. By November, British troops had advanced just 12 kilometres into no-man's-land. Volunteers began to dwindle, so the British government declared that all fit, healthy men between the ages of 18 and 41 had to go off and fight.

In 1917, the USA joined the Allies. In response, the German army launched a huge attack on the Western Front. For a while they were successful, breaking through the trenches briefly, but they were eventually forced to retreat. By autumn 1918, with its people starving and troops exhausted, the German government had to face the fact that they had been defeated. When the guns finally fell silent, the First World War, described at the time as the 'War To End All Wars', had claimed more than 20 million casualties, both soldiers and civilians.

THE EASTER RISING

1916

While the First World War raged across Europe, Ireland was busy battling its own war. Following the disaster of the potato famine (see page 90), the majority of Irish people desperately wanted a greater say in how their country was run.

Ireland was split, however, into two camps. The mainly Protestant North wanted to be ruled by the government in London, but the Catholic South wanted independence from Britain and 'Home Rule' – which was the freedom to rule themselves.

To try and solve the problem, in 1914, Britain drew up plans that allowed Ireland a government of its own. However, when the First World War broke out, the plans for Home Rule were put on hold.

The Irish Republican Brotherhood

For a while, tension between the two sides eased as both Protestant men from the north of Ireland and Catholic men from the south went off to fight in France. Some Irish nationalists (supporters of an independent Ireland), however, thought it was the perfect opportunity to take matters into their own hands.

During the Easter of 1916, members of a group called the Irish Republican Brotherhood launched an armed uprising in Dublin. They took over the city's General Post Office and announced a breakaway government. Unfortunately, the English troops arrived to put down the rebellion. While the rebels managed to fight off the British soldiers for five days, eventually they were forced to surrender, and the leaders were executed by firing squad. The Easter Rising, as it became known, had failed, but the Irish people, furious at how harshly Britain had dealt with them, became more determined than ever to be independent.

LIFE ON THE HOME FRONT
1914 – 1918

The First World War was very different to any other war Britain had ever fought. This wasn't just because of the number of soldiers who died in it, or the appearance of new and deadlier weapons. It was also because of the way it affected life at home. While the war raged in Europe, the people back in Britain were expected to do their bit to help – this became known as fighting on the Home Front.

Women Workers

Before 1914, there were very few jobs open to women – they mostly worked as servants or in factories. However, with most of Britain's young men away fighting, women found they were needed to keep the country going.

Many took up jobs that they would not have been allowed to do before, including working in offices, working on the land to produce much-needed food, and driving buses around the country.

For the first time, women were allowed to do dangerous jobs, such as making weapons, building ships for the navy, and working in coal mines. Though not allowed to actually fight in the war, many women worked as nurses in hospitals near the front line or drove ambulances filled with wounded soldiers.

During the war, the people of Britain had to cope with dwindling food supplies because German submarines attacked British ships bringing food into the country. In order to ensure essential supplies of meat, sugar, butter, cheese and margarine did not run out, food rationing was introduced in the last year of the war. This meant that each person was only allowed to buy a limited amount of food.

Bombings at Home

It wasn't just soldiers on the front line in France who were killed in the war – people at home were also in the firing line. In 1915, two German airships (called Zeppelins) flew over the English Channel on a bombing mission, killing four Britons. It was the first of more than 50 air raids on London and the east coast of Britain.

Did You Know?

There were people in Britain who weren't keen to support the war effort. Some 16,000 people called conscientious objectors (or Conchies), refused to fight on the front line because they disagreed with the idea of fighting any war.

All Change

When the war ended in 1918, it was all change again. Rationing came to an end, and women were encouraged by the government to give up their new jobs so that returning soldiers had work to come home to. Nevertheless, these women workers during the First World War had changed the role women played in British society forever, making it possible for them to win the right to vote in government elections later in 1928.

BETWEEN THE
WORLD WARS

THE EMPIRE SHRINKS

--------------------- **1916 onwards** ---------------------

The years after the First World War kept both politicians and map-makers busy because the British Empire began to shrink, as its colonies enjoyed greater freedom.

Independence for Ireland

Ever since the Easter Rising (see page 103), many Irish people wanted greater independence. A group named Sinn Féin (which is Irish Gaelic for 'We Ourselves') wanted to drive the British out, and organized a military force called the Irish Republican Army (IRA). In response the British sent in a group of ex-soldiers, nicknamed the Black and Tans because of uniforms they wore, who responded to acts of violence by the IRA savagely.

To end the violence, a treaty was negotiated between the British government and Sinn Féin which made southern Ireland an Irish Free State – this meant that it would have some powers to rule itself. Six counties of the nine that made up Ulster in the North were later made part of Britain. This compromise wasn't enough, however, and fighting continued with a civil war in the south. Eventually, an independent Éire (the Irish name for Ireland) was established in 1937.

Breaking Free from Britain

Further afield, other countries were seeking independence. In 1931, Australia, New Zealand, South Africa and Canada were given the right to govern themselves. These countries joined the British Commonwealth of Nations (an organization established to promote trade and peace around the world). India and Pakistan did not gain independence from Britain until 1947 (see page 119), however, and many of Britain's African colonies did not become free from British control until the 1960s and 1970s.

THE NOT-SO-ROARING TWENTIES
1920s

The end of the First World War, unfortunately, did not signal the end of tough times for Britain. While the government had promised soldiers that they would return to 'a land fit for heroes', things didn't go to plan.

Home Sweet Home

A nasty strain of flu broke out in the trenches on the front line in France in 1918. It was known as Spanish Flu (despite having probably spread from the USA), and soldiers coming home at the end of the war brought the disease back to Britain.

The first outbreak of Spanish Flu appeared in Glasgow, Scotland, where sufferers were kept away from other people, in an attempt to contain it. Despite this, the disease quickly spread through the population of Britain. More than a quarter of a million people died in Britain from Spanish Flu and an estimated 25 million people were killed worldwide.

As if that wasn't bad enough, the war had been expensive and Britain was left bankrupt. Many soldiers returned to find they had no work.

Slowly, however, as the people of Britain began to recover from the effects of Spanish Flu, the economy began to recover, too. As life in Britain was starting to improve, people were more determined than ever to put the war behind them and have fun. A new type of music called jazz swept the nation, and jazz clubs opened up where people could try out the Charleston – a new, fast dance step. British people everywhere began to enjoy more free time. They went to the seaside on holiday and listened to broadcasts from the newly formed British Broadcasting Corporation (BBC) on their radios. Membership rocketed of groups for young people such as the Girl Guides and Scouts, while audiences watched the adventures of Hollywood stars, such as the comic actor Charlie Chaplin, on the big screen. This time was called the roaring 20s.

Not everyone shared in the good times, however. Coal miners called a General Strike in 1926, to protest about poor pay and conditions. The strike failed as miners were eventually forced back to work for lower wages and even longer hours.

The Great Depression

When the American economy crashed in 1929, as a result of what is known as the Wall Street Crash, the roaring 20s came to an end. Overnight, millionaires lost all their money and economies collapsed across the world. In Britain, people stopped buying things, and millions became unemployed as shops and businesses shut down. The difficult decade that followed would eventually lead to another world war.

WHY DOES THAT MAN LOOK SO GLUM, HAS NO ONE TOLD HIM THE WAR IS OVER?

UNEMPLOYED AND HUNGRY

FASCISTS IN BRITAIN
1930s

The hopeful mood of the 1920s soon gave way to severe gloom. The monarchy faced crisis in 1936 when Edward VIII gave up the throne to marry the American divorcée Wallis Simpson, and mass unemployment during the 1930s made life miserable for millions in Europe. Some people turned to extreme solutions.

Extremist Ideas

Fascism (an extreme form of politics that believes in having only one ruler, called a dictator) became increasingly popular as a solution to bring an end to suffering across Europe. A fascist political party led by a man named Benito Mussolini had already seized power in Italy, and Adolf Hitler and his extremist party, the Nazis, was voted into power in Germany. The Nazis' political posters blamed Jewish people for the world's problems and used them as a scapegoat (a group to blame), in order to gain support.

However, it wasn't only in Germany and Italy that fascism was becoming popular. In Britain, Oswald Mosley founded the British Union of Fascists (BUF). Like the Nazis, Mosley blamed Jewish people for Britain's problems. In 1936, he claimed that membership levels to the BUF had reached 50,000.

Mosley organized a parade along Cable Street, London. Wearing black shirts, thousands of BUF followers appeared, but they quickly came face-to-face with thousands of opponents. The parade became a riot and the fascists fled. A few months later, the government passed a law banning people from wearing political uniforms and outlawing private armies. This move marked the end for the BUF, but Britain was about to feel the full force of fascism from not very far away … Germany.

THE SECOND WORLD
WAR YEARS

CHAMBERLAIN'S PEACE PLAN
1937 – 1939

Adolf Hitler and his fascist Nazi party came to power in Germany in 1933. Hitler had big ambitions to expand German frontiers, and he started building up Germany's military strength.

Desperate to avoid another war, the British Prime Minister, Neville Chamberlain, decided to follow a policy of appeasement (which meant giving in to reasonable requests from Hitler in an attempt to stop a war breaking out). Unfortunately, his plan had a major flaw – Hitler wasn't reasonable.

After Hitler marched into Austria without too much trouble in 1938, it was clear that he would soon annex (which means take possession of) a part of Czechoslovakia called the Sudetenland. Chamberlain immediately flew to Munich, Germany, to meet with Hitler and try to stop him. Chamberlain returned to Britain waving a signed agreement and declared: 'I believe it is peace in our time.' He had got Hitler to agree to stop any further aggression in Europe, in exchange for control of the Sudetenland.

Broken Promises

Hitler kept his promise – but only for about six months. After sending tanks into the rest of Czechoslovakia, Poland was next in Germany's sights for invasion. Britain promised to help the Poles if they were invaded. And sure enough, when the German army crossed the Polish border, Britain declared war on Germany on the 3rd September, 1939. This marked the beginning of the Second World War – a war that involved many countries and lasted for six, long and bloody years.

SIR WINSTON CHURCHILL
1874 – 1965
(Prime Minister 1940 – 1945 and 1951 – 1955)

When Winston Churchill took over from Chamberlain as Prime Minister in May 1940, Britain was in serious trouble.

The first few months of the war had seen hardly any fighting and people in Britain began calling it a phoney war. Then, in April 1940, the Germans unleashed Blitzkrieg (a series of lightning attacks on the Netherlands, Belgium and France). The German army then began to push through into France. Outnumbered and outgunned, the French surrendered after just six weeks.

Churchill sent thousands of British troops to fight in France. They were quickly forced back by the German army onto the beaches of Dunkirk in northern France, from which they had to be rescued. With only the English Channel, a narrow strip of water, between them and the Nazis, Britain needed to defend itself from invasion … and fast!

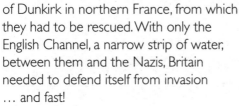

WINSTON, MY HERO!

Churchill's Challenge

Churchill was already 66 years old when he became Prime Minister. His action-packed life, as a politician, soldier and journalist, made him perfectly prepared for the job.

Using inspirational speeches, he united the nation and was often compared to a British bulldog because of his tireless and 'dogged' determination to protect Britain from attack.

Churchill made Britain feel powerful enough to defeat the Nazis, with phrases such as, '… we shall fight on the beaches, we shall fight on the landing grounds, we shall fight in the fields … we shall never surrender.' He became famous for adopting the V for Victory sign (a 'V' sign made using the first and second fingers). Churchill's efforts to fight the Nazis helped bring an end to the Second World War in 1945.

Did You Know?

When Churchill was a boy, he was very naughty at school. One of his school reports said of Winston, 'He cannot be trusted to behave himself anywhere.'

THE BATTLE OF BRITAIN
July – October 1940

By the spring of 1940, Hitler's Nazis were just across the English Channel. Britain prepared itself for attack. Before invading by sea, however, the Germans had to control the skies.

Aerial warfare had come a long way since the First World War, when pilots took random shots at each other with rifles. Both sides now had planes equipped with machine guns.

The Royal Airforce (RAF) had fighter planes called Spitfires and Hurricanes, and the Germans had their own type of fighter plane

SPITFIRE

HURRICANE

called the Messerschmitt BF 109. The problem was, the RAF's planes were outnumbered more than three to one by the German Airforce (called the Luftwaffe). The stage was set for the Battle of Britain.

At the beginning of July 1940, German bombers attacked British ships and airbases. RAF pilots engaged in deadly fights which took place in the skies above the south coast of Britain. Between 1st July and 30th October 1940, the RAF lost 900 planes and the Luftwaffe

MESSERSCHMITT
BF 109

lost 1,700 planes. Britain's allies sent pilots to boost RAF numbers, while support crews worked non-stop to repair damaged planes. Despite this, the British side was struggling.

Things looked bleak until the Luftwaffe suddenly changed tactics – they began to bomb civilians. With German planes focusing on bombing the British mainland rather than gunning down RAF planes, the British quickly gained the upper hand by shooting down more German planes. As a result, Hitler was forced to abandon his invasion plans – the Battle of Britain had been won and the RAF pilots returned as heroes.

Britain's Secret Weapon

The Germans had in fact planned to destroy the RAF in just four days, but they hadn't counted on Britain's top-secret weapon – radar. Strong radio signals were sent out across the English Channel, and radar equipment could then pick up the presence of all planes flying in the area. This early warning system gave the RAF a vital advantage during the Battle of Britain.

THE BLITZ BOMBINGS
7th September 1940 – May 1941

The 7th September 1940 was a date no Londoner would forget. The evening began with the wail of sirens warning of an air raid, then a distant drone as 900 German planes flew over London.

Soon bombs rained down on the city, and this continued almost every night for nine months. The bombings became known as the Blitz, which means 'lightning' in German.

Blackouts and Bunkers

Prime Minister Churchill sheltered from the bombings in a concrete bunker, and families with gardens were given structures made of steel called Anderson shelters. Others were forced to head to underground station platforms to shelter. To make it harder for German bombers to spot targets in the city, the government ordered a complete blackout – this meant people hung heavy curtains up and street lights and traffic lights were switched off.

The Blitz killed around 43,000 people and wounded many more, but the loyal King George VI and his wife refused to leave London. Their visits to Blitz victims made them very popular.

THE WAR ENDS

1944 – 1945

In 1944, the fortunes of the Allied forces continued to improve. People began to feel that, with luck on their side, the war could be over by Christmas.

America and Britain were determined to try and end the war. They planned an attack on German-occupied France. Cleverly, the British fooled the Germans into thinking that the invasion was aimed at Calais, in northern France. A pretend force was even constructed in Kent using fake tanks and aircraft. Then, on 6th June 1944, an order to attack Normandy (a spot further north along the coast of France) came as a total surprise to the Germans. This attack is now known as D-Day.

Thousands of soldiers landed on the Normandy beaches. The first wave of US troops (known as GIs) were met by German machine guns, and 2,000 died, but the Allies pushed on. Faced with the Allies' tactical fighting, the Germans began to retreat, and soon surrendered France. The Allied troops marched towards Berlin.

Russian troops advanced from the East of Europe. When they were just metres from the bunker he was hiding in, Hitler realized he was beaten and shot himself. On 8th May 1945, the Allies accepted Germany's surrender. The day was named Victory in Europe Day (VE Day), but British and US troops were still fighting for their lives in far-off Japan. In August 1945, the Americans dropped devastating nuclear bombs on the Japanese cities of Hiroshima and Nagasaki. The Japanese surrendered and the Second World War was over.

Victory was celebrated wildly, but soon details of the Holocaust (the systematic murder of the Jews by the Nazis) became public. Leading Nazis were imprisoned, put on trial and sentenced to death at what is called the Nuremberg trials.

RECENT HISTORY

INDEPENDENCE FOR INDIA
1947

The cost of rebuilding the shattered economy after the Second World War meant that Britain's days as a colonial power were well and truly over.

In India, people had been struggling for independence from British rule for many years, and they grew increasingly determined. A man named Mohandas Gandhi became a national hero for organizing non-violent protests against British rule. Shot by an extremist assassin, he is often called Mahatma Gandhi, Mahatma meaning 'great soul'.

India finally gained independence from Britain in 1947. Anxious to avoid a bloody battle for power between the main religious groups (the Hindus and the Muslims), the country was divided in two. Part of it became an independent Hindu state and kept the name India, while part became a separate Muslim country, and was called Pakistan. Unfortunately, this plan for a peaceful future didn't work, as millions of people were uprooted and thousands died fighting to stay where they were.

Gradually, more colonies around the world followed India's example and became independent from Britain.

Multicultural Britain

In an attempt to rebuild the economy after the war, the British government began encouraging workers from overseas to work in Britain. In June 1948, a ship called the SS *Empire Windrush* docked at Tilbury docks in London with nearly 500 Jamaicans on board. They were soon followed by people from all over Africa and Asia, and their arrival marked the start of Britain's multicultural society.

119

THE SWINGING SIXTIES
1960s

By the end of the 1950s, the people of Britain had begun to recover from the effects of the Second World War. Rationing had ended, free healthcare was available to all, and Elizabeth II, a new, young queen, was on the throne. Hopes were high of a bright, happy future.

Power to the People

Young people believed they had the power to change the world and many rebelled against their parents' old-fashioned views.

London became the capital of cool as the teenagers hanging out on Carnaby Street and the Kings Road created new fashion and styles that quickly spread around the world. During the 1960s, a British designer made very short skirts called 'minis' fashionable, and four young men from Liverpool formed a band called *The Beatles*. They became the most famous band of all time.

As the decade rolled on, old rules and beliefs were constantly challenged. TV shows poked fun at politicians for the first time, the death penalty was abolished, and a new law made it easier for couples to get divorced. In 1966, England celebrated when its national team won the football World Cup, beating West Germany 4 – 2.

THATCHER AT WAR

(Prime Minister 1979 – 1990)

In 1979, Britain elected its first female prime minister. Margaret Thatcher came to power when Britain's economy was struggling. Determined to pull the country out of trouble, her decisive leadership style soon earned her the nickname the Iron Lady.

Changing Britain

Thatcher believed that people shouldn't rely on the government to look after them and that individuals should work hard to make money for themselves. She wanted Britain to change. She sold off big industries, previously owned by the government, to private companies. She introduced taxes that rewarded the rich.
The economy did improve, but when unemployment figures rose, her policies became very unpopular. Before she could face her critics, however, she found she had a real war on her hands.

On 2nd April 1982, an army from Argentina invaded the Falkland Islands, which lay just off its coast in the south Atlantic Ocean. The Falklands Islands were one of Britain's last remaining overseas territories. Thatcher sent a large military force to get the invaders out. The Argentinians were defeated, and the islands remained British.

After the war, Thatcher made a plan to close down 20 of Britain's coal mines. The miners went out on strike and violent clashes took place between the police and strikers, but after a year of protesting the miners were forced to go back to work. She then attempted to introduce a poll tax (which means both rich and poor have to pay the same amount of money to the government). Riots broke out in protest on the streets of London. Eventually, the Iron Lady became so unpopular among the people of Britain and her own political party, she was forced to resign by her own MPs in Parliament.

THE END OF A MILLENNIUM
1990s

As the twentieth century drew to a close, there was no sign of progress slowing. Scientists were discovering new ways to fight diseases, the Internet gave people a new way of communicating, and the popular use of mobile phones saw the creation of a whole new language – txting! In addition, power within the United Kingdom also changed dramatically.

Peace in Northern Ireland

For many years, the Catholics living in the north of Ireland believed they were being treated badly by the Protestant authorities in charge. The tensions between Catholics and Protestants had exploded into violence. British troops were sent in to restore order, but their actions had the opposite effect. On 30th January 1972, British soldiers shot dead 13 unarmed protesters – the tragic event became known as Bloody Sunday.

The troubles continued for almost 30 years, and many people were killed in bombings and shootings. Finally, on 10th April 1998, both sides signed the Good Friday Agreement, in which they agreed to work with each other and share control of the government of Northern Ireland. There seemed a real chance of peace in Ireland at last.

Devolution

The people of Scotland and Wales wanted more say in how they were governed. In 1999, they were granted devolution, which meant that instead of decisions being made by the Parliament in London, power was handed over to two newly created assemblies – the Scottish Parliament and the Welsh Assembly – where they could run their own affairs and make their own decisions.

A NEW MILLENNIUM

2000

As Big Ben struck midnight on 31st December 1999, fireworks lit up the night sky. Britain had entered a new millennium, and everyone was excited about the future.

Building the Future

The twenty-first century was marked by the building of the Millennium Dome in London and the Science Centre in Glasgow. The world became concerned about the effects on the environment caused by humans, particularly changes in the world's climate. In Britain more than £2 billion was spent on buildings and environmental projects all around the country to mark the millennium. The glass domes of the Eden Project (the world's largest greenhouse), were added to Cornwall's landscape.

In 2005, London celebrated wildly again as it won the opportunity to stage the Olympic Games in 2012.

And the new millennium has only just begun …

AETHELRED THE UNREADY
EDMUND IRONSIDE
CANUTE THE GREAT
HAROLD I
HARDICANUTE
EDWARD THE CONFESSOR
HAROLD II
WILLIAM I
WILLIAM II
HENRY I
STEPHEN (MATILDA)

1016 1035 1040 1042 1066 1087 1110 1135 115

HENRY VII
EDWARD V
EDWARD IV
RICHARD III
HENRY VI
HENRY V
HENRY IV
RICHARD II

1461 1422 1413 1399 137

1509 1485 1483

HENRY VIII
EDWARD VI
MARY I
ELIZABETH I
JAMES VI/I
CHARLES I
OLIVER AND RICHARD CROMWELL

1547 1553 1558 1603 1625 1649 16

GEORGE V
EDWARD VII
VICTORIA

1910 1901

1936

EDWARD VIII
GEORGE VI

1952

ELIZABETH II

124

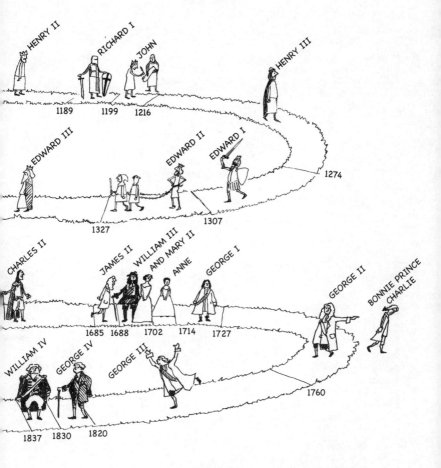

A ROYAL TIMELINE

Follow the winding road to see all the kings and queens that have ever ruled England. The dates show when their reigns began and ended.

INDEX